"Benjamin Conner has written a groundbreaking book that seeks to install a disability perspective to mission studies. The book also suggests that missiology might bring some insights to disability studies. Using examples from the world of the Deaf and the cognitively disabled, as well as other disabilities, Conner has written an enlightening but also soul-searching work of importance."

Lennard J. Davis, distinguished professor of English and disability studies at the University of Illinois at Chicago

"As a Quaker and disability scholar, I found this to be a fascinating and useful read. Among other important topics, Conner provides an excellent discussion of evangelism with Deaf people and people with intellectual disabilities. The author helps us understand both the challenge and the opportunity of a fully inclusive church."

Tom Shakespeare, Norwich Medical School, University of East Anglia

"Ben Conner is an important emerging voice within the field of disability theology. In this book he once again opens up fresh space for reflection on disability and how it relates to the theology and mission of the church. This is a significant book that not only reveals Conner as a top-notch practical theologian, but, if read and acted upon, will truly make a difference to church and society."

John Swinton, professor in practical theology and pastoral care at the University of Aberdeen

D0916247

DISABLING MISSION, ENABLING WITNESS

Exploring Missiology Through the Lens of Disability Studies

BENJAMIN T. CONNER

IVP Academic
An imprint of InterVarsity Press
Downers Grove, Illinois

InterVarsity Press
P.O. Box 1400, Downers Grove, IL 60515-1426
ivpress.com
email@ivpress.com

InterVarsity Press® is the book-publishing division of InterVarsity Christian Fellowship/USA®, a movement of students and faculty active on campus at hundreds of universities, colleges, and schools of nursing in the United States of America, and a member movement of the International Fellowship of Evangelical Students. For information about local and regional activities, visit intervarsity.org.

Scripture quotations, unless otherwise noted, are from the New Revised Standard Version of the Bible, copyright 1989 by the Division of Christian Education of the National Council of the Churches of Christ in the USA. Used by permission. All rights reserved.

While any stories in this book are true, some names and identifying information may have been changed to protect the privacy of individuals.

Content in chapter two adapted from Benjamin T. Conner, "Enabling Witness: Disability in Missiological Perspective," Journal of Religion and Disability *19, no. 1 (2015): 15-29, is used by permission of Taylor & Francis.*

The poem "Culture Shock, Crip-Style" by Laura Hershey (1962–2010), poet, writer, activist, is used courtesy of www.laurahershey.com.

Drawings throughout the book are used courtesy of the artist, Kristen Peyton.

Cover design: David Fassett
Interior design: Beth McGill
Images: © Godong/UIG / Bridgeman Images

ISBN 978-0-8308-5102-7 (print)
ISBN 978-0-8308-8568-8 (digital)

InterVarsity Press is committed to ecological stewardship and to the conservation of natural resources in all our operations. This book was printed using sustainably sourced paper.

Library of Congress Cataloging-in-Publication Data
A catalog record for this book is available from the Library of Congress.

P	23	22	21	20	19	18	17	16	15	14	13	12	11	10	9	8	7	6	5	4	3	2	1
Y	37	36	35	34	33	32	31	30	29	28	27	26	25	24	23	22	21	20	19	18			

To

Darrell Guder

and to

the memory of Dick Woodward

my mentors

Contents

Preface

I have been writing different parts of what feels like the same book for over a decade now. The process began when my experience with a group of young people with disabilities challenged the relevancy of my doctoral dissertation (*Practicing Witness*, 2011). It continued as I ministered to and with them and as they helped me to imagine a different kind of youth ministry (*Amplifying Our Witness*, 2012), and it now finds expression in this book. I humbly offer this work as a foundational contribution to a new conversation that brings disability studies and mission studies into dialogue about the witness of the church. I am hopeful that others will carry this work forward by refining and expanding it.

I am thankful for the many people who have provided feedback, pushback, and encouragement through this process. Early on, I was supported by a research assistant at Western Theological Seminary, Luke Soderstrom, who continues to explore the connections between disability and theology as a perpetual student. Four different Deaf people (scholars, pastors, and innovators) gave me valuable feedback: Kirk VanGilder, Tom Hudspeth, Chad Entinger, and Noah Buchholz. Bradley Nassif helped me navigate my engagement with Orthodoxy. And there were many others: from mission studies, Darrell Guder; from mission studies and disability studies, Amos Yong, who also served as an editor for this volume; from practical theology and disability studies, John Swinton; Randy Smit offered his poetry; Tom Boogaart offered his experience and wisdom; David Komline provided his expertise in American religious history for chapter three; Kristin Johnson and Jeff Monroe offered their careful editorial eyes; and the Friend residents from Friendship House offered their stories and perspectives. The Summer Institute on Theology and Disability provided a space to work through some of the ideas in this book in the form of plenary session presentations and workshops. My students in our Graduate Certificate in Disability and Ministry provided stimulating and generative conversations. Kristen Peyton (www.kristenlied.com) helped me demonstrate the importance of moving beyond words to communicate by creating sketches. Thanks also to Taylor and Francis for permission to use extensively "Enabling Witness: Disability in Missiological Perspective" in chapter two (informaworld.com) and to those who keep Laura Hershey's work and impact alive (laurahershey.com) for allowing me to use her poem "Culture Shock, Crip-Style."

Finally, special thanks go to the Conner children (Tommy, Victoria, Taylor, and Tessa), who endured my present-absence at times while I contemplated and wrote what follows. And thanks to my wife, Melissa, who is always my partner in *coram Deo*: life lived before the face of God.

Benjamin T. Conner
Pentecost Sunday 2017

Introduction

Megan is a thirty-four-year-old woman with cerebral palsy and a significant cognitive impairment who lives in a group home. She is barely verbal, difficult to understand, and, oddly, when she does speak, says everything at least twice in direct succession. She works a few hours a day at McDonald's during the week cleaning up the dining area. On weekends, she goes to church with us. She can't read, so she makes unusual noises during the songs and the recitation of the Apostles' Creed. Her friend Seth, who has Down syndrome, now comes with her, and they always sit near each other. Once when we were out of town, Megan went to church by herself. Her phone made noise during the service, and she was unable to turn it off. She left.

Do you think you know Megan?

Let me try again.

Megan is a resident at Friendship House, a residence on the campus of Western Theological Seminary where seminary students share housing with young adults with intellectual disabilities. She delights in her housemates, and they are her best friends. She sometimes exercises, prepares meals, or creates artwork with the seminary students. On World Down Syndrome Day this past year (always March 21 to symbolize the value of the extra, or third copy of, the twenty-first chromosome in people with Down syndrome), four of the Friendship House Friend residents were looking forward to being acknowledged and celebrated.[1] Megan does not have Downs, but her friends wanted to make sure she was included. When my wife pointed out that Megan didn't have Down syndrome, they insisted, "Megan has Downs." Megan nodded her head vigorously and repeated in

---

[1] Residents of Friendship House with disabilities have taken on the identity of "Friends" or "Friend residents."

affirmation, "Yes, I do . . . yes, I do." Why should she be excluded yet again, this time because she has the "wrong" disability?

She has difficulty communicating verbally and knows it, so in an effort to make sure you can understand what she is saying, she tends to say things at least twice. Every day during the work week, Megan takes public transportation to her job. Once a week she rides horses at a therapeutic riding center.[2] On her way to work, she often texts her friends the emoji of a hamburger, and when it is time to ride, she texts an emoji of a horse. On the weekends, she joins my family at church (and texts us an emoji of a church to let us know she is there and waiting for us), and she is an important part of our community of

[2]For more on therapeutic riding, see the Professional Association of Therapeutic Horsemanship International (PATH Intl.) at www.pathintl.org or Renew Therapeutic Riding Center at www.renewtrc.org.

*At points throughout the following chapters, the reader will find artwork created for the book by the artist Kristen Peyton and intended to supplement the ideas communicated verbally. Please use them to engage other ways of knowing and reflecting on the intersection of missions studies and disability studies.

witness. Though she can't read, she participates in all aspects of the worship service and offers habituated responses to the music and the recitation of the Apostles' Creed.[3] Megan has a contagious enthusiasm about church and emits a profoundly joyful and largely nonverbal witness to being included in the body of Christ. When she invited her friend Seth to attend church with her, of course he came. Everyone wants to be loved and included; everyone is looking for a place to belong. Soon after joining us at church, Seth was baptized.

One Sunday when we were out of town, Megan attended church by herself. She sat in the balcony where we often sit together. No one sat close to her. During the songs, no one found the correct pages in the hymnal for her. At some point during the service, her phone began to buzz, and she was unable to turn it off. People around her "shushed" her and looked at her in a way that she interpreted as harsh and angry. No one helped her. She began to cry. No one comforted her. She quickly left church, ran home, and cried. In the three years we have known her, Megan and her friends from Friendship House have the chance to gather and share highs and lows from the week with my wife and each other. In that time she has had only two lows. One was when my son stopped by McDonald's when she was working; he didn't see her, so he did not greet her. The other low was when her congregation failed her: they didn't make room for her, didn't value her contribution to the church, and didn't seem to want her witness.

It should be obvious that Megan is not suffering because of her cerebral palsy or limited intellectual development. In fact, she is generally one of the most joyful people I know. She does, however, suffer when she feels unwelcomed, excluded, or like she doesn't belong. Don't we all? We must complexify the common-sense belief that all people with disabilities suffer as a consequence of their impairments. Unfortunately, disability and suffering are frequently paired in the relatively few seminary courses that engage the lived experience of disability and in books and curricula that address disability from a faith perspective.

---

[3]Mary McClintock Fulkerson notes how people communicate and receive information in ways that are embodied and habituated. She draws on social anthropologist Paul Connerton to reflect on ways we ritually or habitually know. Megan has "a knowledge and a remembering in the hands and in the body." Mary McClintock Fulkerson, "Interpreting Situations: When Is 'Empirical' Also 'Theological'?," in *Perspectives on Ecclesiology and Ethnography*, ed. Pete Ward (Grand Rapids: Eerdmans, 2012), 133. McClintock Fulkerson draws on Paul Connerton, *How Societies Remember* (Cambridge: Cambridge University Press, 1989), 95.

I don't want to over-interpret Megan's life and appropriate her experiences in an instrumental way to make my points. Much of my retelling of her story is my attempt to allow her to "speak for herself" when words are difficult for her and to allow her to offer a word of challenge to the church. I want to acknowledge that Megan's involvement at church, my familiarity with her, and my awakening to her indispensability as a part of a witnessing community are among the many experiences that led me into the type of theological inquiry found in this book.

Through various communicative modalities, Megan conveyed her delight in attending church with our family, and *her* Spirit-enabled witness prompted Seth to want to join the church. Megan participated in the congregational practice of Christian witness.

Her friend Seth was recently baptized. Seth shares Megan's enthusiasm for church, and while he functions on higher social and intellectual levels than Megan, Seth also lacks the capacity for abstraction that is required to cogitate on deep theological truths. What did he understand about the sacrament? Was the event, in his mind, as much a cause for a party as it was about union with Christ? Does he really understand the Apostles' Creed, which he recited in confirmation of his baptism? Seth certainly knew that he felt loved, and he responded in the way that the community set forth. One of the most important aspects of Seth's liturgy of baptism might not have been his understanding of the event but rather the vow of the congregation members to commit themselves before God to Seth's spiritual nurture.

Seth was asked, "Will you be a faithful member of this congregation, and, through worship and service, seek to advance God's purposes here and throughout the world?" Seth responded "yes" to what he understood to be an invitation to join a community where he felt welcomed. Seth took his place as an ordained (baptized) member of the congregation. By virtue of his baptism he is called to participate in God's ongoing redemptive work in the world and to bear witness to that work, just like Megan. But how will he be able to live out his baptismal identity? Certainly Seth, like all Christians, has received gifts of the Spirit. And I know Seth to have many other characteristics and capacities that he could employ in service of this mission. Still, he is limited intellectually and has a small sphere of social interaction. The clue to Seth's being shaped and supported in his role as a member of the body of Christ is found in the congregation's response. The congregation stands and receives the charge (in the form of a question):

> Do you promise to love, encourage, and support
> *these brothers and sisters*
> by teaching the gospel of God's love,
> by being an example of Christian faith and character, and
> by giving the strong support of God's family
> in fellowship, prayer, and service?[4]

Seth's desire to be baptized provided the congregation with an opportunity to revisit their doctrine of baptism, and it might add a fresh perspective from which the practice of baptism can be more fully appreciated. Seth enters a community of faith just like everyone else—he doesn't have all of the spiritual gifts for the edification of the church, but he has some of them. Like the rest of us in the community of faith, he is not independent but rather interdependent on the Spirit and others in the community for his growth in the life of faith. While he has not yet and might never pass through some of the anticipated stages of physical, cognitive, and psychosocial development, Seth comes into the Christian community with all he needs to be a disciple. His baptism, like every baptism set within the acknowledgment of the Spirit at work and within the confession of a community, bears witness to this fact. Seth's baptism reminds the congregation of what is true of all baptisms—they are more about *God* knowing us and equipping us than they are about knowing exactly what *we* are doing, choosing, or proclaiming.

MY LOCATION

I am a professor of practical theology at a denominational seminary who, along with the others in this community, is invested in preparing the next generation of men and women to lead the church in mission. I do not at this point have a recognized disability and acknowledge the challenge of writing on the subject when I am not disabled. I am an outsider to the experiences of exclusion and discrimination that so many people with

---

[4]Reformed Church in America, "The Order for Profession of Faith and Baptism of Youth and Adults," accessed March 11, 2018, images.rca.org/docs/worship/OrderProfessionBaptism.pdf.

disabilities face.[5] At the same time, I have shared and continue to share life with many friends with disabilities and have found that the concept of disability and the perspectives of people with disabilities can unmask biases and values in our culture that push against human flourishing. Embarrassingly and with great consequence, those biases exist neutrally and go uninterrogated in our churches, seminaries, and divinity schools. In my role as a professor, I have come to recognize that the mere presence of a person with a disability on the campus and in the classrooms at a seminary can make people reconsider received biblical interpretations, theological dogma and formulations, and pastoral practices that we had thought were settled and had become ossified in curriculum. Ultimate questions ranging from creation to *telos* ("What does it mean to be made in the image of God?"; "What are the qualifications of a minister?"; "How are disabilities and eschaton related?") must be revisited and reformed in light of the lived experience of disability.

Examining how disability is constructed and represented in society is of utmost importance for people called together to bear witness to the kingdom of God. We need to [dis]able discipleship and theological education, by which I mean we must expose the ways in which we inhere biases against people with disabilities in every aspect of our life together. We need to do this for the sake of forming disciples in ways that stimulate their theological imaginations toward enabling the witness of their congregations.

How might this happen?

In the process of encountering perspectives of people with disabilities and studying disability theory, students might come to embrace their own disabilities, hidden and visible, and find new energy and perspective from them. When students are in relationship with other students and instructors who have disabilities, the elastic and porous category of disability, as a means of predetermining where someone falls on an ability-disability continuum, will be transcended. Instead of disability being a disqualifying category for participating in theological reflection and pastoral practice, disability will be viewed as a unique point of reference from which new insights

---

[5]I will alternate between the European phrasing "disabled persons," which highlights the social aspect of disability, and the North American "persons with disabilities," which is intended to emphasize the personhood of those with disabilities.

are gained and practices are reformed and refined. Disability scholar Brenda Jo Brueggemann explains that "disability enables insight—critical, experiential, cognitive, and sensory,"[6] so unlocking that insight by acknowledging it, making room for it, and nurturing it by providing discussion platforms and conversation partners enables the sort of theological education that will support congregations in their mission. Disability, rather than being something that gets in the way of a theological education and must be overcome in order to be properly formed for ministry, can provide a perspective from which students can better understand the human condition, doctrines and texts, pastoral skills, and congregational witness.

SUMMARY

The twin purposes of this book are to stimulate a conversation between disability studies and theology (particularly mission studies) around a vision of the entire body of Christ sharing in the witness of the church, and to imagine how we might [dis]able Christian theology, discipleship, and theological education for the sake of enabling congregational witness. In the chapters that follow I prepare the way for a dialogue between mission studies and disability studies by introducing theoretical tools and conceptual categories for [dis]abling from both fields, provide concrete examples of the process of [dis]abling, and propose some ways that our congregational witness is enabled when people with disabilities are involved.

Here is how I will proceed. In part one of the book, two chapters set the stage for the discussion to follow by introducing the two primary conversation partners: disability studies and mission studies. The first chapter, "An Introduction to Disability Studies for Mission Studies," introduces the concept of disability and some of the core themes of disability studies and explains their relevance for theology and mission. It addresses the cultural situatedness of disability and explores how the concept and experience of disability can provide a means for critiquing cultural norms and values that reduce our vision of humanity. I argue that taking the experiences of those

---

[6]Brenda Jo Brueggemann, "An Enabling Pedagogy" in *Disability Studies: Enabling the Humanities*, ed. Sharon L. Snyder, Brenda Jo Brueggemann, and Rosemarie Garland-Thomson (New York: The Modern Language Association of America, 2002), 321.

with disabilities seriously can both enrich congregational ministry and witness and demonstrate how addressing the challenges associated with disability is a matter of justice and reconciliation. The second chapter, "Introduction to Mission Studies: A Disability Perspective," introduces readers to the field of missiology and proposes the missiological concepts of *missio Dei*, indigenous appropriation and contextualization, and Christian witness as potential frameworks for liberating and [dis]abling witness. These missiological tools, I contend, are fitted for preparing temporarily able-bodied people to recognize and appreciate the contributions of people with disabilities in the ministry and witness of the church.

In part two, three chapters draw on the concepts introduced in part one and offer examples of enabling witness through [dis]abling mission studies and theology. Chapter three, "'Deaf to the Ways of God'?" provides a positive interpretation of the often negatively construed phrase in a way that is oriented toward "Deaf gain" rather than hearing loss. This chapter provides a history of Deaf culture in the United States through a missiological lens that connects Deaf culture directly to nineteenth-century evangelistic efforts. It also addresses ways in which Deaf culture, theology, and ministry pose challenges to the practices of evangelism and witness.

Chapter four, "Intellectual Disability and Our Iconic Witness," explores ways that intellectual disability differs from other disabilities and proposes an understanding of evangelism and witness grounded in an appreciative appropriation of Orthodox iconography. My intent is to expand and challenge popular conceptions of witness and demonstrate how people with little or no capacity for abstraction or logical thinking participate in Christian witness.

Chapter five, "[Dis]abling Theological Education to Enable Witness," turns our attention to the setting of theological education and attempts to answer the question, "As a theological educator, how can I participate in [dis]abling theological education for the sake of enabling witness?" I survey the current state of theological studies with respect to the lived experience of disability, develop concepts introduced earlier in the book, and introduce heuristic tools such as de-familiarizing, de-stabilizing, disrupting, and dislocating as means of critiquing and [dis]abling current practice. Finally, I propose a way forward in terms of presence (people with disabilities must be present in all aspects of theological education), intention (the human experience of disability must be directly engaged), and dimension (the human experience of disability must be acknowledged by every field and discipline) for enabling theological education and witness. An epilogue closes the book.

PART I

Setting the Stage

In the following chapters I will set the stage for a conversation between disability studies and mission studies by introducing the dialogue partners to each other. There are many different ways in which one could represent a field of study. For example, mission studies involves contextual analysis, theology, and history, and touches on and draws on many of the social sciences, especially anthropology. Evangelical missions scholar Charles van Engen lists forty-eight separate cognate disciplines with which missiology intersects in its attempt to "describe, understand, analyze and prescribe the complex nature of mission."[1] Each area of emphasis could inform and be challenged by disability studies. My engagement with mission studies will be targeted and guided by the following questions: What concepts or practices from mission studies are most suited to work alongside disability studies to support the flourishing of people with disabilities? What missiological issues are raised by the lived experience of disability?

---

[1]See Charles Edward van Engen, *Mission on the Way: Issues in Mission Theology* (Grand Rapids: Baker Books, 1996), 19n3.

Disability studies is equally broad in range and foci, as I will explain below. My guiding questions for engaging disability studies are: How might disability studies help missiologists to better understand and address the human condition? In what ways can disability studies open missiologists to the many embodied ways that congregations participate in God's mission?

Given the limits of my inquiry, it would be impractical (and impossible) to attempt a comprehensive introduction to either mission studies or disability studies. Alongside the breadth of the fields, both disciplines involve contested boundaries with respect to the scope of the field and often competing interests. This results in very different understandings of whether one is faithfully representing the field. The following two chapters will avoid such intramural battles and instead offer an introduction to each field of study that will enable them to gaze through each other toward the task of enabling witness.

1
· ·

An Introduction to Disability Studies
for Mission Studies

In 1988 our portable church was meeting in a Catholic school gymnasium. On this particular Sunday morning, the gym was not available to us to use as our sanctuary because the floor of the gym was being treated, so the church set up in the cafeteria. Signs led us around the outside of the massive structure to a set of concrete stairs that led up to the cafeteria. As Duncan wheeled around the front of the building to the side stairs, it became clear to everyone, especially to him and his parents, that Duncan was going to have a difficult time getting into church. In that pre-ADA world, Duncan's motorized wheelchair faced several concrete stairs with no ramp or lift.[1] Those around Duncan began to feel at once awkward and guilty, so they hastily considered how to get Duncan into church. But I don't remember anyone consulting Duncan. The solution was for me to carry Duncan up the stairs and to have a few other people carry his heavy motorized chair. I picked Duncan up, but I don't remember asking his permission. At the top of the stairs and back in his chair, Duncan was gracious, but I don't remember him coming back to church.

Duncan was objectified by well-meaning people, and this episode represents the way many churches engage persons with disabilities. The church wants to serve and help, but it has no idea how and tends to do things for people with disabilities rather than with them. There was no sense in my encounter with Duncan that he might not want to be picked up. There was no sense that getting him into church was vital because he might have a

---

[1] The Americans with Disabilities Act is a civil rights legislation that, among many other things, requires the facilities of government-funded entities to be accessible to wheelchair users.

contribution to make that the church needed. Evangelism and mission in
our churches often follow the same approach—evangelism has disability
impairments in view and assumes the person with disabilities needs services
and ministry. Churches seldom consider what people with disabilities might
contribute to the congregation and even less frequently imagine that
someone with a disability could possibly be the minister.

Duncan Borland had multiple sclerosis (MS) and died over twenty years
ago due to complications related to the disease. After attending MIT, where
he played water polo, he attended Union Theological Seminary in Richmond,
Virginia (now Union Presbyterian Seminary), and was ordained a Presbyterian minister in 1990. He was the first Mission Road Developmental
Center chaplain and concurrently served as a beloved associate pastor at
Morningside Ministries in San Antonio, Texas, where he lived until his
death. In 1994, Duncan Borland was honored as the Disabled Worker of the
Year in San Antonio. But how would I ever have imagined any of that? He

was just a disabled guy I needed to get up some stairs so he could attend my church. He needed access, and we gave it to him, right?

Last year Terry DeYoung, coordinator for the Reformed Church in America (RCA) Disability Concerns, guest taught my Ministry and Margins class at Western Theological Seminary. He spoke about his experience of living with a disability, gave a summary of the kind of work that is being done in RCA churches with people with disabilities, and answered questions regarding disability and inclusion in congregational settings. One student asked what people with disabilities in general think about a certain subject. Terry wasn't sure how to respond. He politely addressed the question by beginning, "I can't speak for all people with disabilities, but I think . . ." The question highlighted the underlying assumption, even among sensitive and engaged seminary students, that disability is a homogeneous concept and that one person with a disability can speak for all others.

"Disability" is a designation with a broad spectrum of referents that is constantly under negotiation. It is at times a label applied to people against their will, marking them as somehow defective, incomplete, or medically or psychologically pathological. At other times, the label is welcomed as an explanation and provides an avenue to resources and educational support that leads to access to goods and experiences people would otherwise be without. In particular, persons with invisible or hidden disabilities or impairments that often can't be discerned by observation (many mental health issues, chronic fatigue syndrome, debilitating pain, epilepsy, some traumatic brain injuries, cystic fibrosis, deafness, etc.) can find a diagnostic label explanatory, legitimating, and comforting. As disability scholar Tom Shakespeare explains, "Diagnosis can lead to better understanding of the problem and to access to appropriate support mechanisms: resource allocation is label-led."[2]

"Disability" is also, alternatively, a *badge* or self-selected marker of identity. For example, self-identified "crips" who embrace their embodiment and reliance on wheelchairs or persons on the autism spectrum who embrace their neuro-diversity are not seeking a "cure."[3] Instead, they are asserting the

---

[2]Tom Shakespeare, *Disability Rights and Wrongs, Revisited*, 2nd ed. (London and New York: Routledge, 2014), 96.

[3]The term *crip* is insider language for the disability community and represents an effort to control and recast the derogatory term *cripple*.

value of their differences and the indispensability of their perspectives and experiences for any full account of the human experience. Disability can be a very important identity marker for some people.[4]

Consider, for example, the issues raised by the reception of Shakespeare's *Disability Rights and Wrongs*.[5] In that groundbreaking work, Shakespeare, a scholar and advocate who has a disability, critiqued the British strong social model of disability, explained below, as inadequate. He contended that for all the benefits of the social model, which rightly highlights the social construction of disability and pushes against conceptions of disability as personal and pathological, it fails to address the reality of the human experience of impairment. As he explains, "Disability results from the interplay of individual and contextual factors. In other words, people are disabled by society and their bodies."[6] What was the response to his critique? A series of largely negative reviews of Shakespeare's work was penned by leading advocates of the social model of disability in a significant disability journal that cast his book as "an attack on British disability studies and the disabled person's movement."[7] An article also questioned whether Shakespeare is really even disabled or simply "physically distinct," as with dwarfism. The article continued to assert that to the disability movement, "Shakespeare is no longer disabled but disabling."[8] Who gets to decide whether Tom Shakespeare is disabled?

THE CURIOUS CASE OF JULIA

Disability identities are complex. People with disabilities are often defined by others in terms of one feature: the perceived disability or impairment. Julia Watts Belser, an assistant professor of Jewish studies in the Department of Theology at Georgetown University, lives in the intersection of many different identities and negotiates many labels and badges. (In fact, I have just given you one: professor.) She contends, however, that the advocacy, affinity, or interest group that might pay her and reimburse her travel to speak at a conference on

---

[4]See Shakespeare's discussion of labels and badges in *Disability Rights and Wrongs*, 95-97.
[5]Shakespeare, *Disability Rights and Wrongs*. I use Shakespeare as an example because I draw on his work in the coming chapters.
[6]Ibid., 2.
[7]See *Disability and Society* 22, no. 2 (March 2007): 209-34.
[8]Tom Koch, "Is Tom Shakespeare Disabled?," *Journal of Medical Ethics* 34 (2008): 18.

the issues and concerns that touch on one aspect of her identity do not dictate her identity. She is, in her own terms, "a queer disabled woman" preferring to use disability-first language to talk about her cerebral palsy.

Julia is at once a minority as a woman, a minority as a person in a wheelchair with cerebral palsy, a religious minority as a Jew, a minority within Judaism as a female rabbi, and a sexual minority who claims the designation "queer." Recently, at the Summer Institute on Theology and Disability, she recovered another label or badge, that of "rider," when she rode a horse for the first time since before she was a wheelchair user (twenty years earlier). Zen, a retired dressage horse, had been ridden moments earlier by a young man with Down syndrome who had no previous riding experience and low muscle tone in his core. A seasoned therapy horse, Zen dutifully followed his rider's instructions and loped around the perimeter of the arena and between cones, advancing and halting on command. However, when Julia sat on Zen, the horse immediately recognized what the wheelchair had obscured to others, that Julia was a rider. Zen rounded, tucking in his head and rear, raising his withers and flexing his core muscles as he rotated his ears backward to receive commands. Though Julia has little use of her legs for controlling Zen, the horse detected her strong abdomen, steady seat, and advanced reining. Julia's chair was set aside for the moment as the horse became her legs, and she experienced the intimate connection between human and animal that can only be gained through participating in the practice of horsemanship. Zen was also impacted by the encounter—Zen was enabled to be the horse he had been in the past. At that moment Julia was still a disabled, queer, Jewish woman—and everyone wanted to be her.

DISABILITY STUDIES AND DISABILITY

Disability studies is a multidisciplinary and interdisciplinary field that examines the construction and function of the concept of disability in society as a socio-political, medical, and cultural phenomenon. According to disability scholar Simi Linton, it provides "an organized critique on the constricted, inadequate, and inaccurate conceptions of disability that have dominated academic inquiry."[9] And in Ronald Berger's estimation, disability

---

[9]Simi Linton, *Claiming Disability: Knowledge and Identity* (New York: New York University Press, 1998), 3.

studies is "vital to an understanding of humankind."[10] Disability studies will be our partner as we explore the experience and interpretation of disability and the implications of disability for the theology and witness of the church.

People with disabilities, if abstracted as a group, can be conceived of as the largest multicultural minority group in the United States, an open minority group most people will likely enter against their will through accident, disease, or the natural process of aging. It is a group that includes a collection of people who can be found in every class, race, ethnicity, and economic circumstance. That fact that around 19 percent of the US population, or approximately 56.7 million people, has a disability suggests that nearly every person in the America is touched by it.[11] So what is disability?

Perhaps one could begin with a definition such as that offered by the World Health Organization (WHO) or the Americans with Disability Act of 1990 (ADA). Those definitions read:

> WHO: Disabilities is an umbrella term, covering impairments, activity limitations, and participation restrictions. An impairment is a problem in body function or structure; an activity limitation is a difficulty encountered by an individual in executing a task or action; while a participation restriction is a problem experienced by an individual in involvement in life situations.[12]

> ADA: The term "disability" means, with respect to an individual (A) a physical or mental impairment that substantially limits one or more major life activities of such individual; (B) a record of such an impairment; or (C) being regarded as having such an impairment.[13]

The WHO suggests that over a billion people worldwide have some form of disability according to their definition.

In both definitions, the concept and reality of disability is ascribed to individual or social factors, but all attempts to circumscribe disability fail.

---

[10]Ronald J. Berger, *Introducing Disability Studies* (Boulder, CO: Lynne Rienner, 2013), 3.

[11]United States Census Bureau, "Nearly 1 in 5 People Have a Disability in the U.S., Census Bureau Reports," July 25, 2012, www.census.gov/newsroom/releases/archives/miscellaneous/cb12-134 .html. Nearly everyone is touched by disability in the sense that either you or someone close to you will have a disability at some point.

[12]World Health Organization, "Disabilities," accessed March 11, 2018, www.who.int/topics/dis abilities/en/.

[13]U.S. Equal Employment Opportunity Commission, "Titles I and V of the Americans with Disabilities Act of 1990 (ADA)," www.eeoc.gov/laws/statutes/ada.cfm.

These definitions attempt to differentiate between "disability" and "impairment" and struggle to navigate the spaces between a biomedical model of disability, where the "disability" is considered a pathology or a deficit of the person (John is a person with a disability); the American social model of disability, where John is a member of a minority group (again, using person-first language, John is a person with a disability); and the British strong social model of disability, in which the disabling condition is a social construction imposed on the person (making John a disabled person). If a disability is primarily an individual deficiency or deficit related to impairment, as the biomedical model suggests, then the way forward for addressing the "problem of disability" is to invest in developing more reliable diagnostic tools, emphasize the search for cures, and support the work of rehabilitation. If disability is bound up in identity politics, and people with disabilities are primarily to be understood as a minority group, then the problem of disability should be addressed through civil rights legislation. If a disability is fundamentally a social construct, then, to quote Michael Oliver, "disablement has nothing to do with the body."[14] We must address physical and attitudinal barriers, and unmask and tackle unjust social structures and practices, in order to make environments and physical spaces more accessible. According to Deborah Creamer, a theologian who has a disability, medical and social approaches to disability highlight significant features of disability, but neither the medical model nor either social model of disability captures the variability and volatility of human embodiment and the complexity of the lived experience of disability.[15]

The poem below by Laura Hershey touches on the complexity of disability that Creamer references. Hershey (d. 2010) was a writer, poet, disability rights activist, and consultant. She was a self-identified "crip." To Hershey the term *crip* was a badge, a way of taking ownership of her identity as a wheelchair user that challenged negative assessments of her that were embedded in the dismissive label "cripple." Her poems are witty and visceral— they allow readers to "feel" the experience of living in an able-oriented world

---

[14]Michael Oliver, *Understanding Disability: From Theory to Practice* (London: Palgrave Macmillan, 1996), 41-42.
[15]Deborah Beth Creamer, *Disability and Christian Theology: Embodied Limits and Constructive Possibilities* (Oxford: Oxford University Press, 2009).

with the challenges associated with spinal muscular atrophy. In the poem below, Hershey relates her experience of culture shock as someone who has worked hard to navigate the ableism of the United States.[16] She demonstrates that she is not as disabled as some perceive but finds herself in a culture where she is foreign, even to herself. She does not have the supports she has come to depend on and that represent a sense of home for her. Her poem highlights the complexity of disability, touching on the medical model and impairment effects, the social model and accessibility issues, and crosscultural factors.

Culture Shock, Crip-Style

I breathe in
a chaos of odors, scarcely filtered,
a noxious bouquet.
Throat muscles tense,
push short breaths through drying tissue,
sounds barely strong
enough to pass the blue paper
masking my nose and mouth.
The language I speak here,
fed by this fetor, sounds foreign to my Chinese friend, listening so hard,
leaning toward me on the bus;
sounds foreign to my American friends,
wincing behind their own masks;
sounds foreign to my own ears.
Emerging,
my words are
lost,
exertion wasted in a roar of motor and wind.
I pay a price to be here;

---

[16]See Fiona Kumari Campbell, "Ability," in *Keywords for Disability Studies*, ed. Rachael Adams, Benjamin Reiss, and David Serlin (New York: New York University Press, 2015), 12-14. "A disability studies critique of 'ableism' takes the focus away from disability as a self-contained designation. Ableism denotes the ideology of a healthy body, a normal mind, appropriate speed of thought, and acceptable expressions of emotion. Key to a system of ableism are two elements: the concept of the normative (and the normal individual); and the enforcement of a divide between a 'perfected' or developed humanity and the aberrant, unthinkable, underdeveloped, and therefore not really human" (13).

to plunge myself
into this dense, toxic air;
to traverse this rough land.
In China
I become
more disabled
than I am.
The wheelchair I left at home,
unwelcome in China—too heavy for lifting, defiant of dismantling
—beckons more than my home itself.
Swift, fit, the humming motor—responsive to every pucker and puff,
to every course I bid—
holds my autonomy for safekeeping.
Left behind, it leaves a rift
between decision and
movement.
In this lighter, simpler chair,
I await others' presence, energy, and will.
I speak more weakly here.
I move less.
Travel always stretches, revises
the traveler's self-definition;
it aggravates and violates mine.
This journey makes me
what I am not
back home, though thought to be:
ill, reliant, mute, confined;
more disabled than I am.[17]

Obviously, it is not possible to be in another's shoes. We can "expand the scope of our sympathies," but we can never experience what it is like to be in another's place.[18] This is part of the problem with classroom simulations of disability. Jim Swan reports that a discussion among disability studies scholars and people with disabilities considered such exercises detrimental

---

[17]Laura Hershey, "Culture Shock, Crip-Style" (1995), www.laurahershey.com.
[18]See Catriona Mackenzie and Jackie Leach Scully, "Moral Imagination, Disability and Embodiment," *Journal of Applied Philosophy* 24, no. 4 (2007): 335-50.

because they focus too much on impairment effects without considering the social construction of disability. Additionally, such exercises offer only a false impression or sense of what it is like to live with a particular disabling condition because the student, when the simulation is completed, can continue life as before. Certainly such exercises can be revelatory and meaningful for some students, but perhaps the experience does more to maintain a "normate" bias when the participant "returns to normal."[19] As my friend April is experiencing as the result of a severe injury to her husband's eye in a woodworking accident, there is no return to normal. Nonetheless, poems such as those of Laura Hershey can move us beyond our intellect and help us to connect with the feelings of others in ways that other mediums might not.

Returning to Creamer, in order to address the complexity of disability, she proposes a *limits model* of disability. This model explains, in summary, that all people have limits and that limits, including the limits related to the experience of disability, are common and unsurprising aspects of the human condition. Disability is simply one of many instances of human limitations.[20] In fact, limits "might even be considered an intrinsic element of being human" and should not be discounted as evil.[21] At the same time, not all limits are experienced or interpreted by the people affected or limited by them as being good.

Though definitions can be helpful for identifying and considering the impact of disabilities, whether sensory, intellectual, or physical, most people tend to think they need no help in identifying a disability—we think we know one when we see one. When disability is so "obvious" or "common sense," people tend to forget how socially embedded notions of normalcy, ability, and disability can be. Crosscultural studies help to dislodge us from our position of certainty.

Historian Kim Nielsen, examining the concept of disability among native North American people groups, clarifies that impaired people in indigenous

---

[19]Jim Swan, "Disabilities, Bodies, Voices," in *Disability Studies: Enabling the Humanities*, ed. Sharon L. Snyder, Brenda Jo Brueggemann, and Rosemarie Garland-Thomson (New York: The Modern Language Association of America, 2002), 283-95. The term *normate* is coined by Rosemarie Garland-Thomson in *Extraordinary Bodies: Figuring Disability in American Culture and Literature* (New York: Columbia University Press, 1997), 8.

[20]Creamer, *Disability and Christian Theology*, 31.

[21]Ibid., 32.

cultures would only be considered disabled if they had weak community ties and lacked reciprocal relationships. Disability was viewed in relational rather than individual, body-centered terms. She explains that a young person with intellectual impairments could be excluded from certain roles in society but may have an important community role as a water carrier. "That was his gift," she explains. "His limitations shaped his contributions, but that was true of everyone else in the community as well."[22] Nielsen's explanation begs the question, Did the young person she describes really have an impairment or disability? It is often the case in preindustrial societies that there are important social roles for people who would be dismissed as unable to make significant contributions in a postindustrial, technological society.

Similar to Nielsen's account of native North Americans, the authors of *Disability and Culture* draw on research among the Kel Tamasheq—a North African nomadic people—to expose the cultural factors involved in designating someone disabled. Their notion of "disability" includes determining factors such as "old age and immaturity (making one physically dependent), illegitimate birth (making one socially anomalous), and ugliness (rendering it difficult to marry)," and they consider among defects or faults "deafness, excessive freckles, protruding naval, absentmindedness and flabby or small buttocks."[23] Clearly, the concept of disability is one that is rooted in a social context.

One need not encounter "exotic indigenous peoples" in order to gain a fresh perspective on the problems surrounding the construction of disability.[24] Disability as a concept has been used in the United States not simply as a medical diagnostic marker or a label for people society deems too limited, or who fall outside the boundaries of normal or are not able enough to fit in.

---

[22]Kim E. Nielsen, *A Disability History of the United States* (Boston: Beacon, 2012), 3.

[23]Benedicte Ingstad and Susan Reynolds Whyte, eds., *Disability and Culture* (Los Angeles: University of California Press, 1995), 6.

[24]The terms and concepts of *exotic* and *foreign* are other ways that people with disabilities have been marginalized in the United States. The terms were used to suggest that people who were immigrating to the United States or who were from less-developed countries were behind in the race of evolutionary development. According to this logic, they were dark, backwards, savages, and so on. As we consider in the chapters to follow, people with Down syndrome were given the designation of *mongoloid* to emphasize their otherness and foreignness, and d/Deaf people were summarily considered unintelligent because they did not share the language of the dominant culture. It was argued, on that basis, that d/Deaf people would never make good citizens.

According to Douglas Baynton, the concept has also been used to justify discrimination against other minority groups by attributing disabling conditions to them, such as irrationality, emotional instability, or physical weakness.[25] Racial inequality, the justification of slavery, and unfair immigration restrictions appealed to such disabilities and suggested some racial or ethnic groups are more susceptible to such disabilities and, therefore, represented bad investments for the future of the country. In Baynton's phrasing, "By the mid-nineteenth century, nonwhite races were routinely connected to people with disabilities, both of whom were depicted as evolutionary laggards or throwbacks."[26] Consider the application of the term *mongoloid* to those persons with Down syndrome—a term used to amplify the otherness, difference, and developmental deficiency of people with an extra copy of chromosome 21.

Similar arguments were used to suppress women's rights. As Bayton explains,

> Paralleling the arguments made in defense of slavery, two types of disability argument were used in opposition to women's suffrage: that women had disabilities that made them incapable of using the franchise responsibly, and that because of their frailty women would become disabled if exposed to the rigors of political participation.[27]

Relatedly, Jana Bennet maintains in a recent publication, "Women are disabled. . . . The very fact of being a woman is a disability."[28] In line with the social model of disability, women's very bodies have historically limited their social participation and roles, have been deemed inferior to male embodiment, and have been considered more prone to sin. In relation to the medical model, aspects of their embodied lives produce "disabling" conditions (birth and menstruation, in particular), and women's bodies have been used to justify paternalistic attitudes toward womanhood.

One particularly helpful perspective on disability is that of Tom Shakespeare, introduced earlier, whose viewpoint carries additional significance

---

[25]Douglas C. Baynton, "Disability and the Justification of Inequality in American History," in *The Disability Studies Reader*, ed. Lennard J. Davis, 4th ed. (New York: Routledge, 2013), 17.
[26]Ibid.
[27]Ibid., 23.
[28]Jana Bennett, "Women Disabled," in *Disability in the Christian Tradition: A Reader*, ed. Brian Brock and John Swinton (Grand Rapids: Eerdmans, 2013), 427-41. See also Rosemarie Garland-Thomson's excellent work *Extraordinary Bodies*, esp. chaps. 4-5.

because he was instrumental in developing the WHO's account and definition of disability. He also has a disability, having been born with achondroplasia, or restricted growth (dwarfism). Describing his own situation, Shakespeare explains that restricted growth is a visible impairment that has an impact (people stare, some things are less accessible) and can cause other potential health issues (gastrointestinal issues and vulnerability to back problems). "I have a spinal cord injury," he explains, "which makes me reliant on a wheelchair, which makes my life much harder, even in a totally accessible environment. I have constant neuropathic pain from the spinal lesion. No amount of civil rights or social inclusion will entirely remove these dimensions of my predicament as a dwarf: they are a predicament, even though my life remains happy and fulfilled."[29] Shakespeare moves the discussion of disability beyond the binary issues of medical models (addressing impairment effects) versus social models (issues of access and legislation). He highlights the involvement of the interaction between intrinsic individual factors and extrinsic and contextual structural/social factors, including even the disposition of the disabled persons toward their impairments or disabilities as a factor impacting thriving.[30] A term for Shakespeare's approach is the *cultural model* of disability, a model that "explores the disabled body's interface with the environments in which the body is situated."[31]

The entire conversation about disability and identity becomes more complex if we consider transability, "the persistent desire to acquire a physical disability and/or to seek the actual elective transition of the body from abled to disabled."[32]

Due to the nature of diagnosing and labeling, the discourse surrounding defining disability prioritizes clarifying differences between normal and abnormal, typical and not typical, able and not able, limited and . . . unlimited? Vulnerable and . . . self-possessed/self-sufficient? Nobody would

---

[29]Shakespeare, *Disability Rights and Wrongs, Revisited*, 86.

[30]Ibid., 74-75.

[31]Rachel Adams, Benjamin Reiss, and David Serlin, "Disability," in Adams, Reiss, and Serlin, *Keywords for Disability Studies*, 9.

[32]Elisa A. G. Arfini, "Transability," *Transgender Studies Quarterly* 4, no. 1 (2017), tsq.dukejournals .org/content/1/1-2/228.full. See also Bethany Stevens, "Interrogating Translatability: A Catalyst to View Disability as Body Art," *Disability Studies Quarterly* 31, no. 4 (2011), dsq-sds.org/article /view/1705/1755.

suggest that an unlimited and self-possessed individual exists. Similarly, there is no such thing as a normal, typical, or entirely able or unable person. My point in all of this is to complexify the notions of disability and personhood so that we can address them anew from the vantage point of the theology and the witness of the church.

DISABILITY AND MISSION

One looks in vain to find a text that addresses disability from the standpoint of mission. From the side of mission studies there are texts on healing and medical mission, and biographies of missionaries who spent time with people with disabilities (in leprosariums, such as medical missionaries Paul and Margaret Brand, for example, or the leper priest Father Damien of Moloka'i), but I have found nothing that looks at the contributions from and perspectives of people with disabilities or that considers how their experiences, perspectives, and insights might inform missiology.[33] From the side of disability studies, what we often find are critiques of missionary practice and messages (witness) as paternalistic and imperialistic. One of the purposes of this book, as mentioned above, is to stimulate a conversation between disability studies and missiology around a vision of the entire body of Christ sharing in the witness of the church. Such a task requires people who are committed not simply to an academic exercise but also to the flourishing of people with disabilities.

Tom Shakespeare laments, "All too often, in my view, Cultural Disability Studies seems more concerned with speaking to academic audiences than in advancing the liberation of disabled people."[34] The missiologist can fall into the same trap. We must be reminded by our progenitors that our theology and engagement with disability studies must contribute to the overall witness of the church in welcoming and working on behalf of the kingdom

---

[33]For examples of this type of research that examine healing or medical mission in light of the mission of the church, see Stanley G. Browne, *Heralds of Health: The Saga of Christian Medical Initiatives* (London: Christian Medical Fellowship, 1985); Hessel Bouma III et al., *Christian Faith, Health, and Medical Practice* (Grand Rapids: Eerdmans, 1989); or Willard M. Swartley, *Health, Healing, and the Church's Mission: Biblical Perspectives and Moral Priorities* (Downers Grove, IL: IVP Academic, 2012). For an example of excellence in this type of research, see Christoffer H. Grundmann, *Sent to Heal! Emergence and Development of Medical Missions* (New York: University Press of America, 2005).

[34]Shakespeare, *Disability Rights and Wrongs, Revisited,* 70-71.

of God. Hence we do well to recall that the entirety of Johannes Verkuyl's significant *Contemporary Missiology* is bookended by his cautionary notes: "Missiology may never become a substitute for action and participation"; and, again, "Never—I repeat, never—will missiology be a sufficient substitute for actual participation in the work of mission."[35] Working for the liberation and flourishing of all people lies at the heart of the mission of God in the world—it is the way we practice our witness. As François-Xavier Durrwell has explained in his important study of the concept of witness,

> Concerned as it is with humanity in its totality and fullness, Christ's resurrection seeks to blaze a trail right to the very heart of terrestrial history; it is the divine movement protesting against all injustice, against the evil of death and sin, and claiming for all human beings the dignity of children of God. The witnesses of Christian hope undertake practical services in overflowing love for human beings, starting now in this earthly life.[36]

Christian witness is a response to a divine call to action in the service of human flourishing for the sake of the kingdom of God. We will have much to consider in later chapters about how disability perspectives and the experience of disability are vital to the witness of the congregation, but the predominant emphasis of this book is how people with disabilities can help the church to reimagine mission and witness. For now, consider for a moment the many ways that the missiologist and congregation can engage issues of liberation and flourishing in the lives of persons with disabilities. If they are to be credible partners of Jesus Christ in his ongoing redemptive work in the world, theologians and missiologists must tackle issues such as unemployment, incarceration, loneliness, poverty, homelessness, and mortality rates—all powers and predicaments that push against human flourishing. What we find when we consider such marginalizing and dehumanizing situations in the United States is that people with disabilities are disproportionately impacted.

As you might imagine, all of the various predicaments addressed above and investigated below are intersectional, meaning that each has an impact

---

[35]Johannes Verkuyl, *Contemporary Missiology: An Introduction* (Grand Rapids: Eerdmans, 1978), 6, 407.
[36]F. Durrwell, "Christian Witness: A Theological Study," *International Review of Mission* 69, no. 274 (April 1980): 125.

on the others in a way that compounds the intensity of the disadvantage. Not all people with disabilities are so vulnerable, but as the numbers below will demonstrate, many are. While we do need to acknowledge the gifts and capacities of people with disabilities in the church—and their gifts and ministries are our gifts and ministries—there are still many people with disabilities who are in precarious circumstances and who need the community, services, and advocacy that a church can provide in the execution of her mission of proclaiming the kingdom of God in word and deed. All of the issues engaged below are found across the spectrum of ability/disability, but as I will demonstrate, the reality of disability amplifies their impact.

EMPLOYMENT

There are many positive accounts of employment for people with disabilities. For example, Microsoft recognized how the standard interview process that elevates the importance and value of social skills may be causing them to overlook talents that are frequently associated with the autistic mind. On World Autism Day, Microsoft announced a pilot program for hiring people with autism that involved adjusting their hiring practices and interview processes to make them more suitable to the 80 percent of people with Autism Spectrum Disorder (ASD) who are unemployed and who are particularly suited to be software engineers or data and operations analysts.[37]

Still, the percentage of people with disabilities who are employed (that is to say, "the percentage of the population aged sixteen and older that are currently employed or actively looking for a job, are not in the military and not institutionalized") trails those without disabilities by a large margin. According to the US Department of Labor Bureau of Labor Statistics, in 2015 17.1 percent of people with disabilities were employed versus 64.6 percent of those without disabilities.[38] Disability rights activist Marta Russell argues that there is systematic discrimination inherent in our economic system against disabled people that cannot be addressed by the provisions of the ADA. Notions of individualism, the idea that all achievement is based on merit, and, relatedly, the conviction

---

[37]Jennifer Warnick, "Unique Microsoft Hiring Program Opens More Doors to People with Autism," Microsoft, February 9, 2016, news.microsoft.com/stories/people/kyle-schwaneke.html. Thanks to my son, Tommy, for leading me to this account.

[38]Bureau of Labor Statistics, "Persons with a Disability: Labor Force Characteristics Summary," June 21, 2017, www.bls.gov/news.release/disabl.nr0.htm.

one can rise as high as one wishes if he or she simply puts in the work (meritocracy) ignore the economic structures and power relationships that sustain employment discrimination. Russell explains, "Civil rights laws envision equal treatment, but do not acknowledge the full impact of competition and efficiency governing capitalist economies. The market transgresses on nearly every liberal right, including the right to a job accommodation."[39] The work of the person with a disability may never match up in the evaluative metrics of purely economic considerations because "both pure economics and liberal civil rights law remedies are based on the 'atomistic individual.'"[40] From the standpoint of theology, such evaluative metrics and individualism are undone by a theological anthropology, as we will explore in chapter four below.

ABUSE AND VIOLENCE

Deinstitutionalization, the movement from the mid-1960s of moving care for people with disabilities from large, often poorly supervised public asylums into independent living or community-based care facilities, was a promising and potentially humanizing movement. However, with people moving out of large, impersonal institutions, a new problem arose—the challenge of monitoring abuse in smaller settings that included similar dynamics of power, isolation, and vulnerability.[41] A 2013 survey, taken by 7,289 people online representing all fifty states, nearly five thousand of whom either had a disability or an immediate family member with a disability (the rest were advocates, service providers, or professionals), revealed that 70 percent of people with disabilities claimed they had experienced abuse. While a comparison to abuse among nondisabled populations would have been helpful, we must still conclude that the numbers are staggering. The abuse could be broken down into the following categories: 87.2 percent verbal-emotional abuse; 50.6 percent physical; 41.6 percent sexual; 37.3 percent neglect; 31.5 percent financial.[42] And 90 percent of those who said they faced abuse communicated that they had faced

---

[39]Marta Russell, "What Disability and Civil Rights Cannot Do: Employment and Political Economy," *Disability and Society* 17, no. 2 (2002): 130.

[40]Ibid., 132.

[41]Nora J. Baladerian, Thomas F. Coleman, and Jim Stream, "Abuse of People with Disabilities: Victims and Their Families Speak Out," 2013 Spectrum Institute Disability and Abuse Project, www.disabilityandabuse.org/survey/survey-report.pdf, ii.

[42]Ibid., 3.

abuse on multiple occasions. Additionally, more than 73 percent of respondents with disabilities replied that they had been victims of bullying.[43]

The Bureau of Justice, analyzing crime against persons with disabilities from 2009 to 2012, found that people with disabilities face nonfatal violent crimes at a rate nearly three times the rate of people without disabilities (sixty per one thousand), and in every racial-ethnic group people with disabilities have a higher violent victimization rate.[44] And, interestingly, a recent study of the media coverage of high-profile police-related killings by the Ruderman Family Foundation came to a surprising conclusion in their executive summary: "Disabled individuals make up a third to half of all people killed by law enforcement officers," and "the media is ignoring the disability component of these stories."[45]

POVERTY

There is a significant "poverty gap" between civilians with and without disabilities living in communities in the United States. Based on the U.S. Census's American Community Survey, the Disability Compendium estimates that gap to be over 15 percent—that is to say, the 2016 poverty rate for persons without disabilities is 11.6 percent, and the poverty rate for persons with disabilities increases to 26.7 percent.[46] Disability is related to poverty in a number of ways, one of them being that due to impairment effects and job discrimination individuals with disability made up only 6 percent of the civilian labor force according to the 2010 U.S. Census. And, in the jobs they had, people with disabilities earned approximately 75 percent of what their coworkers without disabilities made. Beyond that, the kinds of jobs they had

---

[43]Ibid., 32.

[44]Erika Harrell, "Crimes Against Persons with Disabilities, 2009-2012—Statistical Tables," Bureau of Justice Statistics, February 25, 2014, www.bjs.gov/index.cfm?ty=pbdetail&iid=4884. Such abuse has recently come to national attention through the 2017 case of a young man with disabilities in Chicago who was abducted, bullied, and tortured for nearly three days. Doug Stanglin and Melanie Eversley, "Chicago Facebook Live Beating Suspects Charged with Hate Crimes," *USA Today*, January 5, 2017, www.usatoday.com/story/news/2017/01/05/police-charges-soon -suspects-chicago-torture-video/96191382/.

[45]David M. Perry and Lawrence Carter-Long, *The Ruderman White Paper on Media Coverage of Law Enforcement Use of Force and Disability: A Media Study (2013-2015) and Overview*, March 2016, www.rudermanfoundation.org/wp-content/uploads/2016/03/MediaStudy-PoliceDisability_final -final1.pdf, 1.

[46]Institute on Disability, "2017 Annual Disability Statistics Compendium Release," https://disability compendium.org/sites/default/files/user-uploads/Compendium_2017_Final.pdf, 33. The poverty threshold in the US for two adults with two children was $24,563 in 2016; US Census Bureau, "Poverty Thresholds: 2016," www.census.gov/library/publications/2017/demo/p60-259.html.

were lower paying in general (janitor, building cleaner, dishwasher, sanitation worker), with many of the jobs being more dangerous and without health insurance.[47] As Lennard Davis says,

> If it is the case that disability causes poverty, and the poverty likewise causes disability, since poor people are more likely to get infectious diseases, more likely to lack genetic counseling, more likely to be injured in factory-related jobs and in wars, and more generally likely to have a dangerous working environment, then we have to see disability as intricately linked to capitalism and imperialism, or the latter-day version of imperialism that shifts factory work to Third World countries and creates poor and rich nations to facilitate a division of labor.[48]

HOMELESSNESS

Not surprisingly, then, more than 40 percent of the homeless population is composed of people with disabilities. Of course, this is intersectional; it is related also to access to medical care, job security, and the like.[49] Anyone who has spent extended periods of time in a soup kitchen or with a homeless ministry will not be surprised to discover that 20-25 percent of the homeless population has a severe mental illness (compared to 6 percent of other Americans).[50]

INCARCERATION

Historian Kim Nielsen observes that incarceration is "the dominant method of 'care' and institutionalization for poor people perceived to have mental or psychiatric disabilities."[51] People with disabilities, even if they are not incarcerated in jails or prisons, face a kind of incarceration where "isolation and control" masquerade as "care and protection."[52] Professor of disability studies Liat

---

[47]"Workers with a Disability Less Likely to Be Employed, More Likely to Hold Jobs with Lower Earnings, Census Bureau Reports," United States Census Bureau, March 14, 2013, www.census .gov/newsroom/press-releases/2013/cb13-47.html. For more on the causal relationship between poverty and disability, see Daniel C. Lustig and David R. Strauser, "Causal Relationship Between Poverty and Disability," *Rehabilitation Counseling Bulletin* 50, no. 4 (Summer 2007): 194-202.

[48]Lennard J. Davis, *Enforcing Normalcy: Disability, Deafness, and the Body* (New York: Verso, 1995), 85.

[49]Michelle Diament, "More Than Two-Fifths of Homeless Have Disabilities," July 16, 2009, www .disabilityscoop.com/2009/07/16/homeless-report/4153/.

[50]"Mental Illness and Homelessness," National Coalition for the Homeless, July 2009, www .nationalhomeless.org/factsheets/Mental_Illness.pdf.

[51]Nielsen, *Disability History of the United States*, 164.

[52]Liat Ben-Moshe, "'The Institution Yet to Come': Analyzing Incarceration Through a Disability Lens," in Davis, *Disability Studies Reader*, 132.

Ben-Moshe expands the concept of incarceration to include "hospitalization, institutionalization and imprisonment and a fuller understanding of the forces that construct medicalization and criminalization."[53] The consequences of such incarceration for all people, but especially for those with disabilities, is a kind of dehumanization in which their "citizenship and personhood are questioned."[54]

Nirmala Erevelles examines the intersection of race, class, and disability where "incarcerated bodies become profitable commodities in the neoliberal prison-industrial-complex of late capitalism."[55] Erevelles builds on Michelle Alexander's popular and compelling argument in *The New Jim Crow* that underserved, undereducated, poor minority groups are disproportionately sent to prisons, where they become a new lower class of people. If they are released, they face job discrimination, are no longer eligible for certain state and federal support programs related to housing, food, and financial aid, and lose the opportunity to exercise citizenship by voting or serving on juries.[56] Erevelles adds that not only is race a factor in creating the new group, but class and disability are also important factors for understanding the "othering" of the new group. Disability lies at the front end of the "school-to-prison pipeline," she contends, explaining, "the logic of disability (feeblemindedness) as dangerous pathology also implicated in the construction of black men as dangerous (sexual) predators justified the most violent practices of Jim Crow and eugenic criminology."[57]

Beyond young people, the U.S. Department of Justice's Bureau of Justice Statistics confirms that around 30 percent of federal prisoners and 40 percent of local jail inmates report having at least one disability, the most common being a cognitive disability. These percentages are significantly higher than those of the general population. Certainly the cause is intersectional, but the significance of disability cannot be overlooked.[58] Ben-Moshe

---

[53] Ibid., 133.

[54] Ibid., 135.

[55] Nirmala Erevelles, "Crippin' Jim Crow: Disability, Dis-Location, and the School-to-Prison Pipeline," in *Disability Incarcerated: Imprisonment and Disability in the United States and Canada*, ed. Liat Ben-Moshe, Chris Chapman, and Allison C. Carey (New York: Palgrave Macmillan, 2014), 81.

[56] Michelle Alexander, *The New Jim Crow: Mass Incarceration in the Age of Colorblindness* (New York: The New Press, 2010).

[57] According to Michelle Alexander, the school-to-prison pipeline consists of "numerous institutional actions that collectively undereducate and overincarcerate students of color at disparate rates." Ibid., 104. See Erevelles, "Crippin' Jim Crow," 92.

[58] Jennifer Bronson, Laura M. Maruschak, and Marcus Berzofsky, "Disabilities Among Prison and Jail Inmates, 2011–12," Bureau of Justice Statistics, December 2015, www.bjs.gov/content/pub/pdf/

explains how this can be: "Prisoners are not randomly selected and do not equally represent all sectors of society. A disproportionate number of persons incarcerated in US prisons and jails are disabled, poor, and/or racialized." And if people are not disabled upon entering prison, there is a strong chance that they will be disabled while in prison by the environment, as the authors explain, due to "hard labor in toxic conditions; closed wards with poor air quality; emotional, physical and sexual violence; the circulation of drugs and needles; and lack of medical equipment and medication."[59]

CONCLUSION

The church is in a unique position to address the unemployment, abuse, violence, poverty, homelessness, and various incarcerations faced by people with disabilities. Unfortunately, the church has not consistently understood it to be included in its mission and witness in the world to address such concrete and tangible issues as a part of its proclamation of the kingdom of God (Mt 25:31-46). Instead, the church has often uncritically accepted the world's estimation of people with disabilities. Why so many crimes, so much abuse, so much discrimination against people with disabilities? Because people with disabilities are commonly more vulnerable and, to put it bluntly, viewed as somehow less than fully human both outside and within the church. Churches must speak into this issue of righteousness and justice. Graduate theological institutions must expose ableist and normate biases in society and model how to include the gifts and abilities of people with disabilities in their communities for the sake of the church. The following chapter offers one example of how to get the conversation started by introducing mission studies as a conversation partner for disability studies in an attempt to infuse disability concerns into our theological imagination.

---

dpji1112.pdf. Additionally, youth with disabilities (who are served under IDEA—the Individuals with Disabilities Education Act) make up 33.4 percent of the youth in juvenile corrections in the United States, most having emotional or specific learning disabilities. See Mary Magee Quinn et al., "Youth with Disabilities in Juvenile Corrections: A National Survey," *Exceptional Children* 71, no. 3 (2005): 339-45.

[59]Liat Ben-Moshe, Chris Chapman, and Allison C. Carey, "Reconsidering Confinement: Interlocking Locations and Logics of Incarceration," in *Disability Incarcerated*, 16.

2
·····································

An Introduction to Mission Studies
for Disability Studies

As people with disabilities and their advocates encourage faith communities to integrate people with disabilities and their concerns more fully into congregational life, many different conversation partners from across the theological disciplines have supported them. Ethicists (Hans Reinders and Stanley Hauerwas), feminists (Deborah Creamer), liberation theologians (Nancy Eiesland), practical theologians (John Swinton and Benjamin Conner), biblical scholars (Hector Avalos, Sarah Melcher, and Jeremy Schipper), educational theorists (Brett Webb-Mitchell, Barbara Newman, and Erik Carter), practitioners and advocates (Jean Vanier and Jennie Weiss Block), and theological systematicians (Amos Yong, David Pailin, and Tom Reynolds) have contributed their insights and disciplinary perspectives to the issue. Notably absent in this discussion have been offerings from the field of mission studies, or missiology.

Missiology is a term used to refer to everything related to mission, including the history of mission, biblical foundations of mission, theology of mission, theological reflection on the practice of mission, cultural and anthropological studies as they relate to understanding and supporting mission, and strategies for mission. As Andrew Walls succinctly describes it, "The term 'missiology' is used in two related senses: (1) for theological reflection on Christian mission (equivalent to theology of mission, theology of the apostolate or sometimes theory of mission); and (2) more broadly, for the systematic study of all aspects of mission"; in short, missiology is "the systematic study of all aspects of mission."[1] More precisely, missiology is an integrative and multidisciplinary

---

[1]Andrew F. Walls, "Missiology," in *Dictionary of the Ecumenical Movement*, ed. Nicholas Lossky et al., 2nd ed. (Geneva: WCC Publications, 2002), 781.

field of study that is particularly attentive to how interaction with cultures, social traditions, and religious convictions transforms the church through boundary crossing.[2] These two concepts of boundary crossing and church transformation have been priorities for the disability movement, and disability theology in particular as it has sought to support disabled people through practices of liberation and inclusion, and through the recognition of their gifts and value to faith communities. Missiology can provide the perspectives and practices necessary to support disability theology so that the fullness of the gifts and challenges of people with disabilities will be recognized and incorporated into the church's ministry and witness.

Therefore, my purposes in this chapter are to reorient the current discussion of theology and disability around missiological concerns and to promote a vision for the entire body of Christ sharing in the worship and

---

[2]See Stanley Skreslet, *Comprehending Mission: The Questions, Methods, Themes, Problems, and Prospects of Missiology* (Maryknoll, NY: Orbis, 2012), 13.

witness of the church. As I am developing a domestic missiology of disability, I will draw heavily on US missiologists and those who touch on
the Gospel and Our Culture Network discussion.[3] I will also draw on
insights from mission scholars beyond the United States who offer
valuable crosscultural perspectives on the theology and practice of
mission. With reference to the missiological concepts of *missio Dei*, indigenous appropriation, contextualization, and witness, I will demonstrate that diversity and pluriformity (variety of forms or expressions) are
essential to Christian community and witness and include not simply
cultural differences but also differences in embodiment, neurodiversity,
and the full range of human limits and capacities. Finally, I will conclude
with an example of how one missiologist, Lesslie Newbigin, has already
applied a mission-studies perspective to disability. His efforts merit both
appreciation and critique.

WHY MISSIOLOGY?

At the historic 1910 World Mission Conference in Edinburgh, Indian An-
glican Bishop V. S. Azariah critiqued Western mission practices and noted
how in his Indian context Western missionary partners demonstrated paternalism and condescension in their dealings with the "younger churches"
(a term that indicates the paternalism Azariah experienced). He offered the
account of an Indian superintending missionary who, in fifteen years, was
never invited into the home to share a meal with his European missionary
partner.[4] They shared the gospel and the missionary task, he explained, but
did not share their lives (1 Thess 2:8). Consequently, the Western church
missed out on how Indian cultural perspectives could enrich the Christian
tradition because, as Azariah explains, "the Indian nature has aptitude to
develop devotional meditation and prayer, resignation and obedience to
the will of God, the Christian graces of patience, meekness, and humility,
the life of denial of self, the cultivation of fellowship and communion and

---

[3]This discussion was stimulated and influenced heavily by Lesslie Newbigin and developed into
and beyond the seminal text; see Darrell L. Guder, ed., *The Missional Church: A Vision for the
Sending of the Church in North America* (Grand Rapids: Eerdmans, 1998).

[4]V. S. Azariah, "The Problem of Co-operation Between Foreign and Native Workers," in *World Missionary Conference, 1910: The History and Records of the Conference Together with Addresses Delivered
at the Evening Meetings* (Edinburgh and London: Oliphant, Anderson and Ferrier, n.d.), 310.

the practice of the presence of God. These elements of Christian mysticism find a natural soil in the Indian heart."[5]

The Indian people had gifts to bring to the witness of the universal church, but the Western church did not receive the gifts. Finally, to conclude, Azariah challenged the paternalism of Western missions, pleading, "You have given your goods to feed the poor. You have given your bodies to be burned. We also ask for love. Give us *friends*."[6] Despite the fact that Western missionary partners had offered his people so much, because there was no reciprocity or mutuality in the relationship, Azariah felt as though he didn't belong. I have heard the same cries of frustration from people with disabilities. The efforts of the disability rights movement to secure access has the goal of inclusion, and inclusion must give way to belonging in order for the church to be changed.[7]

It would not be unfair to ask, then, if one is invested in liberation, inclusion, and the recognition of the gifts and value persons with disabilities, Why missiology? After all, has not the missionary enterprise demonstrated intolerance for other cultures through imperialist strategies and paternalistic attitudes? Have not missionaries engaged in proselytism, a form of evangelism that prioritizes one historical expression of the faith and imposes it on another people group as the faith that must be uncritically accepted? Have not postcolonial and postmodern critiques exposed Western mission activities as exercises in cultural hegemony? The 1932 "Hocking Report," an evaluation of the missionary enterprise after one hundred years of American mission activity, summarized contemporary assessments of Christian mission by stating, "The three bursts of Christian mission activity, after the first or apostolic epoch, have been with periods of military, exploring or commercial activity." This suggests that the motives, methods, and message of the missionary can never be unraveled.[8] Certainly, this is

---

[5]Ibid., 314. Christine Pohl and Chris Heuertz agree, stating, "At the heart of mission is friendship. God's friendship is a gift available to anyone who is open to receiving it"; in Christopher L. Heuertz and Christine D. Pohl, *Friendship at the Margins: Discovering Mutuality in Service and Mission* (Downers Grove, IL: InterVarsity Press, 2010), 123.

[6]Ibid., 315.

[7]John Swinton, "From Inclusion to Belonging: A Practical Theology of Community, Disability and Humanness," *Journal of Religion, Disability and Health* 16 (2012): 172-90.

[8]William Ernest Hocking et al., *Re-Thinking Missions: A Laymen's Inquiry After One Hundred Years* (New York: Harper and Bros., 1932), 10.

not the case with all expressions of US mission—there are many faithful and inspiring examples of missions and missionaries who humbly engaged other cultures and stood with them together under the blessings and critique of the gospel. Nonetheless, American missions have been justifiably accused of unwittingly uniting Christianity with colonialism and at times promoting capitalism, supplanting civilizations while transferring American culture, and expanding commerce in the name of Christian mission. Missiology is the discipline that allows us to take such charges seriously while at the same time exploring how God has been at work both through and beyond the initiative and actions of the missionaries.

In this chapter I am not trying to make the case that Christian mission or missiology as a field has taken the lived experience of or issues related to disability seriously. I am suggesting, however, that contemporary missiologists, especially those who have attended to crosscultural perspectives and those who were on the receiving end of paternalism, exclusion, and marginalization, have developed theological concepts and practices that can support disability advocates with the task of developing a contextualized disability theology and for reimagining the church's witness.

Stanley Skreslet, who has made several recent contributions to configuring the structure of mission studies, considers missiology a "nexus," or "one of the few places in the curriculum where primary studies of text, history, truth (i.e. systematics), and practice naturally intersect."[9] Elsewhere Skreslet writes, "Missiology is not a recapitulation of the field of theology. Nor is it a new kind of social science or branch of history, although here, too, we find significant degrees of overlap due to the sharing of research methods and topics of mutual interest. The distinctive character of missiology is to be found rather in the way that it integrates what appear to be contrasting concerns."[10] Similarly, historian Mark Noll argues that this "nexus" position affords missiologists an ideal location from which to challenge and support historians because missiologists "already have learned to balance the perspectives of various cultures and to explore the shape of Christian

---

[9]Stanley H. Skreslet, "Nexus: The Place of Missiology in the Theological Curriculum," *Association of Presbyterians in Cross-Cultural Mission Newsletter*, no. 31, April 1998.

[10]Stanley H. Skreslet, "Configuring Missiology: Reading Classified Bibliographies as Disciplinary Maps," *Mission Studies* 23, no. 2 (2006): 198.

contextualization in a variety of widely scattered regions."[11] Missiology, at its best, is an ecumenical and unsettling field of study that applies the wisdom garnered from participation in, and the interdisciplinary study of, God's ongoing redemptive mission in the world to congregational life. Missiology examines the encounter between gospel, culture, and church in a way that puts the sender and receiver together as both respond to the initiating mission of God.

In what follows I will introduce three concepts that have emerged in contemporary missiology in response to critiques of mission that I find particularly applicable to disability studies. First, the theology of *missio Dei*, or mission of God theology, emphasizes that mission is God's initiative rather than the consequence of human striving. *Missio Dei* is the foundational missiological concept for conceiving an inclusive and pluriform church—all that follows depends on the *missio Dei*. Second, by prioritizing *indigenous appropriation* and reception over missionary initiative, and by attending to the process of *contextualization*, missiology safeguards the cultural diversity of Christianity. Finally, in *Christian witness* missiologists recognize the essential pluriformity of Christian presence, proclamation, and activity—all voices, articulations, and manifestations of witness are essential. In the remaining paragraphs I will demonstrate how these missiological concepts, which have grown out conversations with and have supported the identity of marginalized Christians in the former "mission fields," open up fresh pathways for recognizing the contributions of people with disabilities in the church.

Missio Dei

Missio Dei theology developed as a critical concept to distance the notion of mission from the contingent and troubled expressions of missions evident in the colonial missionary enterprise.[12] *Missio Dei* performed an important function for missions, as it continues to do today. It humbles missionaries with respect to their own activities and impact, and it assures us that the

---

[11]Mark A. Noll, "The Challenge of Contemporary Church History, the Dilemmas of Modern History, and Missiology to the Rescue," *Missiology: An International Review* 24, no. 1 (1996): 51.

[12]John G. Flett, *The Witness of God: The Trinity, Missio Dei, Karl Barth, and the Nature of Christian Community* (Grand Rapids: Eerdmans, 2010).

church can point to signs of God's redemptive activity in the world while forsaking the triumphalism that has historically characterized the missionary movement.[13] *Missio Dei*, therefore, is a theological concept that has created the space necessary to affirm the value of missions while at the same time providing a vantage point from which to reevaluate and reframe the notion of mission.

South African mission scholar David Bosch notes that since the 1950s there has been a decisive shift away from understanding mission individualistically in terms of "saving souls," socially as an extension of the benefits of Western culture, or ecclesiocentrically, where the church is both the initiator and the goal of mission. The emerging consensus has been to consider the mission in which the church participates in terms of God's initiative.[14] In this understanding of the mission of God, we can imagine the expansion of the gospel not simply in terms of the geographic area covered by missionaries or the number of adherents converted to the Christian faith. The expansion of the gospel, in terms of the *missio Dei*, acknowledges that the gospel is expanding toward a fuller manifestation as the many different expressions of the Christian faith provide the ecumenical church with a greater understanding of our Lord.

If mission is lodged in God's own cause and enabled through the activity of the Holy Spirit, then the church can expect to be surprised by the activity and witness of God in the world. An important undertaking of mission is discerning what God is already doing in the world; this activity of God sometimes corresponds with human missionary efforts, and it sometimes works despite them. In the words of Nigerian historian E. A. Ayandele, "Even if *you* came to us within the framework of colonialism, and did not preach the Gospel in all its purity, that has not prevented *us* from receiving the Gospel and genuinely living it."[15] If the church's participation in God's mission is dependent on the Holy Spirit and not human initiatives and

[13]Christoph Benn, "The Theology of Mission and the Integration of the International Missionary Council and the World Council of Churches," *International Review of Mission* 76 (July 1987): 390; Johannes Aargaard, "Trends in Missiological Thinking During the Sixties," *International Review of Mission* 62, no. 245 (January 1973): 15.

[14]David Jacobus Bosch, *Transforming Mission: Paradigm Shifts in Theology of Mission*, American Society of Missiology series 16 (Maryknoll, NY: Orbis, 1991), 389-93.

[15]Walbert Buhlmann, *The Coming of the Third Church: An Analysis of the Present and Future of the Church* (Slough, UK: St. Paul Publications, 1976), 171.

capacities or church programs and related strategies, then anyone who can bear the Holy Spirit, regardless of cultural setting, embodiment, intellectual capacity, or social skills, can participate in God's mission. As we will explore below, if God's mission is directed to the ends of the earth and all its inhabitants, then we should expect the church to be diverse and the church's witness to take many forms.

INDIGENOUS APPROPRIATION AND CONTEXTUALIZATION

As missiology has addressed postcolonial critiques of Christian imperialism, one response has been to take the focus off sending organizations and attend to the patterns and processes involved in the indigenous appropriation of the message. As mission scholar Lamin Sanneh contends, Christianity from its origins is a religion that expands by means of translation. In the beginning, that meant relativizing yet promoting certain aspects of its Jewish heritage and destigmatizing and adopting aspects of Gentile culture. This process does and must continue due to the very nature of the gospel. Sanneh therefore shifts the emphasis from the missionaries' activity to the missionary activity of God (the *missio Dei*)—from the missionary's transmission of the gospel to the impact of the gospel on the people through their own agency, assimilation, adaptation, and response.[16] Sanneh reasons further that if Christian history is to avoid being the history of Western religious institutions, it must be animated by a historiography that is "guided by the principles of local agency and indigenous cultural appropriation."[17]

Central to understanding how people and groups appropriate the Christian gospel is the issue of conversion. *Conversion* is a term that refers to turning or reorienting existing thought patterns, practices, and traditions toward Jesus Christ rather than displacing what is there and replacing it with something else. According to Andrew Walls, "Conversion is the turning, the re-orientation, of every aspect of humanity—culture specific humanity—to

---

[16]Lamin O. Sanneh, *Translating the Message: The Missionary Impact on Culture* (Maryknoll, NY: Orbis, 2001).

[17]Lamin O. Sanneh, "World Christianity and the New Historiography: History and Global Interconnections," in *Enlarging the Story: Perspectives on Writing World Christian History*, ed. Wilbert R. Shenk (Maryknoll, NY: Orbis, 2002), 99.

God."[18] Proselytism, in contrast to conversion, makes one cultural expression of Christianity normative and consequently superior to all others, disregarding the necessary social and cultural contexts of the gospel. Proselytism traffics in assimilation: "Assimilation repudiates differences," explains theologian Thomas Reynolds. "It feigns an inclusion of differences that is at best a paternalistic gesture of charity, helping 'those others' get along 'like us'; at worst it is an act of coerced subjugation."[19] Conversion is essential to the process of indigenization. Ghanaian mission scholar Kwame Bediako illustrates the importance of indigenization by referencing the words of African philosopher John Mbiti: "We have to sing the Gospel in our tunes, set to our music, played on our instruments. I speak metaphorically. We must drum it out with our great drums, on our tom-toms, on our waist-shaped drums, for only these can vibrate and awaken entire villages: the violin is too feeble to awaken the sleeping pagans of our society."[20] Proselytism, as implied in Mbiti's account, makes one cultural expression of worshiping God normative and fails to recognize that worship with the violin is itself merely one potential manifestation of responding to God. It is no more faithful, and in this case less evocative and meaningful, than worshiping God with drums.

Unless the gospel finds full expression in a particular culture and separates itself from the culture it received it from, it will be incarcerated in the other culture. The religious adherents, or proselytes in that case, will be, in Andrew Walls's language, "disabled from bringing Christ to bear" on the issues that are of concern to them.[21]

Historically, the ways in which biblical interpretation, theology, and ministerial practices have been taught in seminaries has made expressions of the gospel in disability terms unlikely in a way similar to how paternalistic Western mission practices suppressed the voice of the indigenous cultures

---

[18] Andrew F. Walls, *The Missionary Movement in Christian History: Studies in the Transmission of the Faith* (Maryknoll, NY: Orbis, 1996), 28.

[19] Thomas E. Reynolds, *Vulnerable Communion: A Theology of Disability and Hospitality* (Grand Rapids: Brazos, 2008), 47.

[20] Kwame Bediako, *Theology and Identity: The Impact of Culture upon Christian Thought in the Second Century and in Modern Africa* (Oxford: Regnum, 1992), 311.

[21] Walls, *Missionary Movement*, 52. Using the term *disabled* to represent an inability is the exact kind of language and idea I hope to overcome in this project. But it is important to leave here in order to bring up the problem.

of the "younger churches." Nevertheless, we see people with disabilities appropriating the gospel in their own terms and in ways that reveal new dimensions of the reign and rule of Christ.

One problem with the process of indigenization, however, is that indigenization favors continuity with the past, and "the more the Gospel is made a place to feel at home, the greater danger that no one else will be able to live there."[22] That is to say, the universal gospel can be conceptualized in ways that are so particular that it ceases to bear ecumenical family resemblances with other cultural expressions of the gospel. It can also mix so much with culture that it becomes syncretistic—a gospel of the culture without the ability to call unfaithful, non-Christian practices into question. When this happens, the earthly expression of the kingdom of God, the "city on a hill" that is supposedly welcoming to people and drawing them in the name of Christ, becomes inaccessible on many levels.

While the concept of indigenization helpfully draws on agricultural images and refers to taking root in local soil, Taiwanese mission scholar Shoki Coe contends that the metaphor is largely backward-looking and static. He proposes contextualization or contextualizing theology as a concept that is more dynamic and future oriented—"an ongoing process, fitting for the pilgrim people, moving from place to place and from time to time."[23] The incarnation, he explains, is the "divine form of contextualization," and we respond to that event "through responsive contextualization, taking our own concrete, local contexts seriously."[24] The incarnation is the theological rationale for contextualization; we do not attempt to reproduce the unique Christ event but rather offer human responses that are "provisional and fragmentary witnesses to that divine contextualization of the incarnation."[25] The limited nature of our contextualization suggests that in order to have a fuller expression of the body of Christ, we must make room for many contextual theologies. In Coe's words, "We can welcome with joy the emergence of black theology, and for that matter, yellow theology, and the theology of liberation, for the sake of the true catholicity of the gospel.

---

[22]Ibid., 84.
[23]Shoki Coe, "Contextualizing Theology," in *Mission Trends No. 3: Third World Theologies*, ed. Gerald H. Anderson and Thomas F. Stransky (Grand Rapids: Eerdmans, 1976), 22.
[24]Ibid., 23.
[25]Ibid.

There is no colourless theology. But there is all the joy of the multiple colours mobilized for the beauty of the new heaven and the new earth which God has promised."[26]

We can add to Coe's theologies a variety of disability theologies that are emerging. For example, in the United States, Nancy Eiesland has observed, "For many disabled persons the church has been a 'city on a hill'—physically inaccessible and socially inhospitable."[27] Her attempts at contextualizing the gospel from a disability perspective are generative for people with and without disabilities because they work to dislodge settled theological conceptions and practices and offer guidance for reimagining the Christian life and faith with a fuller vision of humanity (and God) in view. Contextualization is the missiological tool that uproots theology from one context so it can take root and grow in another. Contextualization reminds us, as Andrew Walls has clarified, "Nobody owns the Christian faith. Cultural diversity was built into it from the beginning."[28] The continuing process of contextualizing theology helps us to remember that "no one cultural expression of the religion is exclusive for expressing the fullness of the gospel."[29] There is a notion of contextualization in which the sending culture attempts to shape the message to fit a particular context. That is not what these authors are talking about. True contextualization moves beyond imposing one culture-specific expression of the faith on another group and even beyond outsiders adapting the faith so it fits a particular context. Contextualization emphasizes the fact that local congregations must initiate and sustain the dialogue between gospel and culture. In the words of the disability rights movement, this impulse is shared in the slogan "Nothing about us without us."[30]

What is at stake in contextualization is the fullness of the body of Christ. The very diversity of Christian humanity—young and old, ethnically diverse, with all variations of embodiment—is necessary in order for the church to be complete and bear a credible witness to the world. In the first century, Jew

---

[26]Ibid., 24.

[27]Nancy L. Eiesland, *The Disabled God: Toward a Liberatory Theology of Disability* (Nashville: Abingdon, 1994), 20.

[28]Andrew F. Walls, "The Expansion of Christianity: An Interview with Andrew Walls," *The Christian Century*, August 2-9, 2000, 792.

[29]Sanneh, *Translating the Message*, 74.

[30]James I. Charlton, *Nothing About Us Without Us* (Berkeley: University of California Press, 1998).

and Gentile sat at the meal table together and visibly demonstrated the unifying power of reconciliation, what Walls recognizes as a paradigmatic Ephesians 4 moment: attaining "the measure of the full stature of Christ" (Eph 4:13). "None of us can reach Christ's completeness on our own," he explains. "We need each other's vision to correct, enlarge, and focus our own; only together are we complete in Christ."[31] Contextualization is the guarantor of the cultural plurality of the Christian church.

And contextualization can be upsetting, even terrifying, because while the process brings gains in insight and enrichment to our understanding of the gospel, it also brings discomfort and a sense of loss. In a series of talks given by Lesslie Newbigin to clergy of the Church of South India, later published as the *Good Shepherd: Mediations on Christian Ministry in Today's World*, Newbigin presents us with this challenge:

> We have not been willing to take the risks involved in re-thinking our faith, re-casting it in new terms, so that it takes up and re-interprets whatever in these movements is according to the will of God. We have been too timid, too anxious to make sure that we preserve intact what has been committed to us. We are unfaithful servants, because the treasure committed to us has been given not that we should hoard it, but that we should risk it in the commerce of the world, so that it may make a profit for the Master.[32]

It is through the process of contextualization that we respond to Newbigin's challenge.

At the heart of missiology, then, lies the openness to encounter, to risk change for the sake of enriching and amplifying the gospel, which is ripe for a dialogue with the insights from disability studies and the perspective of people with disabilities. Newbigin writes, "The fact that Jesus is much more than, much greater than our culture-bound vision of him can only come home to us through the witness of those who see him with other eyes. . . . We need their witness to correct ours, as indeed they need ours to correct theirs. At this moment our need is greater."[33] Missional and ecumenical theologian

---

[31] Walls, *Missionary Movement*, 79.

[32] J. E. Lesslie Newbigin, *The Good Shepherd: Meditations on Christian Ministry in Today's World* (Grand Rapids: Eerdmans, 1977), 120.

[33] J. E. Lesslie Newbigin, *Foolishness to the Greeks: The Gospel and Western Culture* (Grand Rapids: Eerdmans, 1988), 146-47.

Darrell Guder concurs: "Neither the church nor its interpretive doctrine may be static. New biblical insights will convert the church and its theology; new historical challenges will raise questions never before considered; and new cultural contexts will require a witnessing response that redefines how we function and how we hope as Christians."[34] Taiwanese mission scholar Shoki Coe adds, "There is no colourless theology. But there is all the joy of the multiple colours mobilized for the beauty of the new heaven and the new earth which God has promised. Or to change the metaphor, all the sounds must be mobilized in the great symphony of the Hallelujah Chorus, to be heard not only in heaven but on earth."[35]

Nancy Eiesland, whose *Disabled God* is a touch point for many discussions of theology and disability, has made much of the marks of Jesus' post-resurrection impairment—Jesus is the disabled God. Positively, she has driven home the point that personhood is fully compatible with the experience of disability. What those marks represent is much more than the fact that Jesus was maimed and therefore shares somehow in the experience of being physically disabled. The marks of Jesus represent the fact that in the person of Jesus, God shared in the human experiences of exclusion, intolerance, injustice, religious and societal persecution and oppression, marginality, and weakness that people with disabilities face. Deborah Creamer, expounding Eiesland's theology, explains that due to his "shared experiences of discrimination and oppression" and "prejudice and exclusion" that are common to disability, one can justify the claim Jesus was, in fact, disabled.[36]

Eiesland employs contextualized theology in her liberation theology of disability and offers the following operational definition: "Contextualization is an authentic process of perceiving how God is present with people with disabilities and unmasking the ways in which theological inquiry has frequently instituted able-bodied experience as the theological norm."[37] Eiesland is certainly correct to discern the critical power of contextual theology. However, according to contemporary mission scholars, contextualization is a much more dynamic, multidirectional, and multivalent process. More than

[34]Guder, *Missional Church*, 12.
[35]Coe, "Contextualizing Theology," 24.
[36]Deborah Beth Creamer, *Disability and Christian Theology: Embodied Limits and Constructive Possibilities* (Oxford: Oxford University Press, 2009), 25.
[37]Eiesland, *Disabled God*, 98-99.

a liberating tool of a minority group trying to secure rights and access, contextualization provides a call to the entire church to grow into maturity and fullness. In this sense, Eiesland's most helpful statement in terms of contextualization is the following: "Our bodies participate in the imago Dei, not in spite of our impairments and contingencies, but through them."[38] All of who we are participates in the image of God as we bear gifts that edify the body of Christ and bear the witness of the Spirit. In disability terms, one could say the body of Christ is not healthy without the infirm; its witness is disabled without people with impairments; it forgets who it is without people with dementia. The insights that Eiesland applies through contextualization to the *imago Dei*, the person of Christ, and the liturgical life of the church can be applied to Christian witness as well when a disability perspective is considered.

CHRISTIAN WITNESS

A Christian witness is a person or a community (*martys*); a Christian's witness is her/his/their testimony (*martyrion*); and Christians witness, that is to say, the individual or community participates in observable proclamation, events, or enactments that communicate something about the reality and consequences of the reign and rule of God.[39] Newbigin also summarizes, "In the New Testament it is clear that the only sign of the Kingdom is Jesus himself. The central task of the Church, as it prays 'Your Kingdom Come!' is to bear witness to him in who the kingdom *has* come, to call all [people] to the U-turn in the mind which we call conversion so that they may acknowledge him as King and join his whole Church in the prayer: 'Come Lord Jesus.'"[40] Witness is thus a biblical and theological concept that is crucial for considering the church's Spirit-enabled missionary presence in the world. Though the specific shape of Christian witness varies by context, it is always centered on the kingdom of God as revealed by the true witness, Jesus Christ, of whom it is said, "For this I was born, and for this I came into the world, to testify to the truth. Everyone who belongs to the truth listens to my voice" (Jn 18:37), and the witness is personally experienced

---

[38]Ibid., 101.

[39]See the discussion of the concept in Darrell L. Guder, *Be My Witnesses: The Church's Mission, Message, and Messengers* (Grand Rapids: Eerdmans, 1985), 40.

[40]Lesslie Newbigin, *Sign of the Kingdom* (Grand Rapids: Eerdmans, 1980), 69-70.

and received through the deposit that guarantees the truth of the witness, the *arabon*, the Holy Spirit—the last article of the creed and the first fact of experience, as Lesslie Newbigin has suggested.[41] In Darrell Guder's estimation, the term *witness* is an "overarching term" that comprehends the "Spirit-enabled" community life, proclamation, and service.[42] The most important ability with respect to Christian witness is the Spirit's ability. This notion of witness explained above is theologically rich enough to include the presence, words, and actions of people of all ethnicities, races, genders, ages, and abilities.

While there are many qualities of this Spirit-enabled witness that are important for the church to consider, there are a few that are particularly germane for considering the relationship between dis/ability and witness. Our starting point is always with the initiative of God. As Guder has crisply stated, "The essence of witness, then, is the gracious action of God that produces such witnesses and their testimony."[43] The action of God is manifested through a witness that is Spirit enabled, involves the communication of a testimony, and cannot be separated from the community that is called by God to bear the Spirit's witness.

Witness is Spirit enabled. The power of the witness's testimony, its impact on those who encounter it, is more a factor of the promise of the presence and power of the Holy Spirit—"But you will receive power when the Holy Spirit has come upon you; and you will be my witnesses" (Acts 1:8)—than it is a matter of the persuasiveness and rhetorical shrewdness of the witness. Scripture testifies, "No one can say 'Jesus is Lord' except by the Holy Spirit" (1 Cor 12:3). Such a declaration relativizes all methods, techniques, and strategies for witness. It should also challenge our conceptions of what it means to participate in the Spirit's witness. The enabling event of Pentecost became the foundation for a movement that crossed all types of boundaries (social, cultural, and physical, and the boundary between faith and unbelief), and it is paradigmatic for all subsequent missionary activity. It is only a church that participates in the boundary-crossing movement of the Holy Spirit that

---

[41]"The Holy Spirit may be the last article of the Creed but in the New Testament it is the first fact of experience"; Newbigin, *Household of God*, 89.

[42]Darrell L. Guder, *The Continuing Conversion of the Church* (Grand Rapids: Eerdmans, 2000), 53.

[43]Ibid., 60.

shares in the mission of God. Human participation in bearing the Spirit's witness is not related in any way to social status, cultural location, or ethnicity; prior credentials, qualifications, or merit; or intellectual capacities, physical attributes, or sensory function. All can participate in the ongoing redemptive ministry of the church by the Holy Spirit. Minister, educator, and disability advocate Brett Webb-Mitchell has explained,

> And in this body, the Spirit of God does not choose to neglect or not be in the life of people whom the world calls disabled, let alone in the distribution of gifts, services, and talents in the body of Christ. None of the gifts of the Spirit are withheld or designated to people based upon one's academic pedigree, or an intelligence quotient score, social adaptation scale, or any other modern day assessment tool.[44]

Human participation in God's redemptive mission is significant and authentic, but for people on all phases of the ability spectrum, it is derivative and relies on a power that is beyond the congregation's nature. As Newbigin explains, "This mission is not simply entrusted to the Church as a human corporation. It is the continuing work of Christ Himself through the Holy Spirit."[45] Importantly, the witness is not simply an activity of the church directed to the world; it is a Spirit-enabled witness directed to the world of which the church is a part. The witness, the announcement of the truth of the kingdom of God, has a transformative effect on both the world and the church.[46] It challenges, changes, and calls them both to live into that for which the church is a sign, instrument, and first fruit. This is Newbigin's terminology. He often refers to the ways in which the congregation represents the reign of God as "sign, instrument, and foretaste" of the reign of God.[47] He writes elsewhere, "The witness of the Church is the sign and instrument, and of which its life is the foretaste" of the coming consummation of the kingdom of God.[48] He reiterates variously that the church is "servant,

[44]Brett Webb-Mitchell, "Educating Toward Full Inclusion in the Body of Christ: People with Disabilities Being Full Members of the Church," *Journal of Religion, Disability, and Health* 14 (2010): 264.

[45]J. E. Lesslie Newbigin, "One Body, One Gospel, One World," *Ecumenical Review* 11, no. 2 (January 1959): 152.

[46]J. E. Lesslie Newbigin, *The Open Secret: An Introduction to the Theology of Mission*, rev. ed. (Grand Rapids: Eerdmans, 1995), 56.

[47]Ibid., 163.

[48]Newbigin, *Household of God*, 145.

witness and sign of the kingdom" and "sign, agent, and firstfruit," even "sign and agent and foretaste of the Kingdom of God."[49] The fact that our witness is enabled by the Spirit means the theological enfranchisement of those who are labeled disabled to be full participants in the church's witness in the power of the Spirit (just like everyone else).

Witness involves the communication of a testimony. Christian witness is borne through many different communicative modalities. Durrwell describes witness as the translation of the mystery of Christ and salvation into "a sign language, its uprising into the visibility of this world."[50] Darrell Guder argues similarly when he contends, "Our theology of the church, summarized under the imperative 'Be my witnesses,' must be open to the enormous diversity of Christian modes of expression and thought."[51] But the theologian who develops the missiological foundations for describing the kind of diversity that can comprehend the many ways people communicate is Pentecostal missiologist Amos Yong.

Yong embodies much of what has become most important in missiology today: Yong is a Pentecostal theologian (one of the expressions of Christianity that is flourishing with the "southern shift" in Christianity's center of gravity) and a leader in the field of Buddhist-Christian studies and interreligious dialogue (he is attuned to our religiously plural society);[52] he grew up as a religious minority in west Malaysia (another embodiment of the life of global Christians); as a child his father pastored a first-generation Chinese

---

[49]See Newbigin, *Foolishness to the Greeks*, 117, 136, respectively, and Lesslie Newbigin, *The Gospel in a Pluralist Society* (Grand Rapids: Eerdmans, 1989) 86-87.

[50]F. Durrwell, "Christian Witness: A Theological Study," *International Review of Mission* 69, no. 274 (April 1980): 131. Perhaps Durrwell is Deaf to the ways of God (understood positively, of course).

[51]Guder, *Be My Witnesses,* 89-90.

[52]See in particular Philip Jenkins, *The Next Christendom: The Coming of Global Christianity* (Oxford: Oxford University Press, 2002). Whereas in 1900 32 percent of the world's population lived in the USSR, Europe, and North America, in 2000 that number had dropped to 18 percent and is projected to be a mere 10-12 percent by 2050. Accompanying these shifts in population are shifts in the center of gravity of institutional Christianity. In 1900 80 percent of the world's Christians lived in the West, but by 2000 only 40 percent of the world's Christians lived in the West. In 1900 only 9 percent of Africa was Christian. By 2000 that percentage had jumped to 46 percent. It is amusing to note that the majority of the world's Anglicans are Africans. In fact Jenkins predicts, based on figures from David Barrett and Todd Johnson, that by 2050 50 percent of the world's Christians will live in Africa and Latin America, with an additional 17 percent in Asia. A typical contemporary Christian, argues Jenkins, is a woman in a village in Nigeria or in a Brazilian *favela*. Christianity is becoming again, in the words of Kwame Bediako, a non-Western religion.

immigrant population in California; and he has a brother with Down syndrome and has contributed to the ongoing discussion of theology, biblical studies, and disability.

As a missiologist, Yong offers a perspective on *missio Dei* and witness rooted in the Pentecost event that is particularly generative for disability theology. Yong develops the concept of a "pneumatological imagination"[53] to refer to a way of understanding God, self, and world that is inspired by the Pentecost event and the Pentecostal-charismatic experience of the Holy Spirit.[54] It is a way of "participating in the fields of force generated by the Spirit's presence and activity" that acknowledges God's active redemptive work in the world by the Holy Spirit and seeks creative ways to join it. A community with a pneumatological imagination recognizes that the church does not own and cannot manipulate the Spirit. The community therefore expects to find the Spirit at work, testifying to truth through many disparate things (e.g., the sciences, other religions, and many modes of cognition and communication) while respecting the integrity and identity of each witness, not conflating them.[55] Through the pneumatological imagination, Yong engages science, the world Christian movement and global theology, religious dialogue, political theory, and disability.[56]

According to Yong, the Holy Spirit is the mode through which the *missio Dei* is animated. "Because the Holy Spirit empowers human witness," Yong explains, "I claim that the pneumatological imagination not only enables human knowing but also directs liberative human activity."[57] As applied to the missionary encounter, Yong continues, "The Christian encounter with

---

[53]He borrowed this term from Lucien Richard, but it has become identified with Yong's body of work.

[54]Amos Yong, *Discerning the Spirit(s): A Pentecostal-Charismatic Contribution to Christian Theology of Religions* (New York: Bloomsbury T&T Clark, 2000).

[55]For more on this see Christopher A. Stephenson, *Types of Pentecostal Theology: Method, System, Spirit* (Oxford: Oxford University Press, 2016), chap. 4, which is devoted to explication of Yong's method.

[56]See James K. A. Smith and Amos Yong, eds., *Science and Spirit: A Pentecostal Engagement with the Sciences* (Bloomington: Indiana University Press, 2010); Amos Yong, *The Spirit Poured Out on All Flesh: Pentecostalism and the Possibility of Global Theology* (Grand Rapids: Baker Academic, 2005); Amos Yong, *Hospitality and the Other: Pentecost, Christian Practices, and the Neighbor* (Maryknoll, NY: Orbis, 2008); Amos Yong, *Theology and Down Syndrome: Reimagining Disability in Late Modernity* (Waco, TX: Baylor University Press, 2007); and Amos Yong, *The Bible, Disability, and the Church: A New Vision of the People of God* (Grand Rapids: Eerdmans, 2011), as representative of his publications that draw energy and perspective from the pneumatological imagination.

[57]Yong, *Theology and Down Syndrome*, 14.

religions today is witnessed to by the many tongues enabled by the Spirit and engaged through the many hospitable practices empowered by the same Spirit."[58] Included among those "practices empowered by the Spirit" are practices of mission as participation in the hospitality of God, practices of mission as seeking peace and justice, and practices of mission as inter-religious dialogue.

At the ecclesiastical heart of Yong's missiological proposal is his com-mitment to the charismatic diversity in the church. As Yong develops in a recent publication, "The many tongues of Pentecost and the many prac-tices of the Spirit of God are the means through which Divine Hospitality is extended through the church to the world, including the worlds of reli-gions, and that it is precisely through such interactions that the church in turn experiences the redemptive work of God in anticipation of the coming kingdom."[59]

He applies this same missional principle to his theology of disability, arguing for visible unity in the body of Christ: "So, against a body of Christ divided between the able-bodied and the disabled, I would suggest a char-ismatic fellowship of the Spirit that blesses and receives blessings from people with and without disabilities equally."[60] Given the democratic nature of the Spirit, with regards to both gifts and witness, Yong can conclude, "The outpouring of the Spirit unleashes many tongues and many senses—many different communicative modalities—to bear witness to and receive the witness of the wondrous works of God. All forms and all types of dis/abilities, then, would be possible conduits for the Spirit's revelatory work, to those who would be receptive of the outpouring of the Spirit."[61] His "many tongues, many senses" approach destigmatizes modes of communi-cation that are typically underemphasized and underappreciated by the church yet are essential to appreciating and amplifying the witness of people across the ability spectrum.

This insight is summarized by Yong as follows: "The many tongues of Pentecost are indicative also of the many different ways in which God both

---

[58]Yong, *Hospitality and the Other*, 129.
[59]Ibid., 100.
[60]Yong, *Bible, Disability, and the Church*, 7-8.
[61]Ibid., 72.

reveals himself and interacts with the various sensory capacities of embodied human beings. This 'many tongues, many senses' hermeneutic also illuminates how God condescends to meet human beings with diverse levels of ability and disability."[62] This is an important point that could be said differently but also critically. Thus, in a provocative book, Sharon Betcher argues, "Rather than blessing corporeal flourishing in all its multiple forms, even when it limps, wheels, and winces, even progressive, liberal theologies focused on Jesus as Healer might be included in what theologian Marcella Althaus-Reid designates as 'decency theologies'—theologies that, given the impetus of modernity, became conflated with middle-class morality and, consequently, begin to discipline bodies into the status quo."[63] Such critiques are important reminders that, in the power of the Spirit, God enables many different modes of flourishing. In line with Amos Yong's pneumatological imagination explained above, Betcher's pneumatology "promotes the Spirit not as the power to rescue and repair according to some presupposed original state or ideal form, but as the energy for unleashing multiple forms of corporeal flourishing."[64]

WITNESS CANNOT BE SEPARATED FROM THE COMMUNITY CALLED BY GOD TO BE WITNESSES

The manifold witness of a community or the unique witness of an individual is often made comprehensible by the life of a community that serves as a hermeneutic for the testimony. Newbigin takes this statement a step further, insisting, "The only hermeneutic of the gospel, is a congregation of men and women who live by it."[65] At the same time, Christian communities are neither self-contained nor self-sufficient—we cannot realistically posit a Christian culture against a broader, un-Christian culture. Indeed, Christians do participate in some fairly isolated social activities (ecclesial practices), but Christians have other social roles in other spheres of living. The interactions and assumptions that are operative in those spheres also impact the activities and attitudes of those people who make up the church. This makes

---

[62]Ibid., 15.
[63]Sharon V. Betcher, *Spirit and the Politics of Disablement* (Minneapolis: Fortress, 2007), 52.
[64]Ibid., 50.
[65]Newbigin, *Gospel in a Pluralist Society*, 227.

the boundaries between a Christian and a non-Christian way of life more permeable than many Christians are comfortable admitting.[66] Fortunately, Christian witness in culture is not a matter of preserving a separated community in unmixed purity that adventures on occasional excursions into the world for the sake of witnessing to it. Instead, "Wherever in our apostolate we *see a convincing demonstration of Christ's solidarity with the world*, we will clearly have to be present *in* this world with solidarity, not just now and then in a sortie from the ecclesiastical enclave only to return thereafter with great great speed, but *permanently*, because we know that as Christians we have our *Sitz im Leben* (life situation) in the world, not in the church. In the world one must live as a 'child of the kingdom, that has been planted on the acreage of the world.'"[67] Put otherwise, witness is a matter of a community that lives in the world in the power of the Sprit and, in Kathryn Tanner's words, situates their Christian practices "in the wider field of cultural life on which they are a commentary."[68]

Tanner's notion of Christian practice being a commentary on "the wider field of cultural life" is another way suggesting that the congregation is a hermeneutic of the gospel, or a way that a congregation practices witness. In order for that commentary or testimony to the gospel to be credible, according to Newbigin, it requires "a congregation of men and women who believe it and live by it."[69] All of the activities of the church (evangelistic work, ministries of service, conferences, etc.) are secondary and must lead to a concrete believing community.

As he has explained elsewhere, the church as the fruit of the kingdom of God is available in foretaste; the power of the Holy Spirit is at work "healing, helping, and releasing"; and witness is borne, beyond itself, to the future fullness of redemption in Christ.[70] The congregation is the concrete community where this testimony happens. The new reality, "the common life (*koinonia*) in the Church" created by the Spirit, is the headwater from which flows both proclamation and service. In fact, this new reality, "the active

---

[66]Nicholas M. Healy, "Practices and the New Ecclesiology: Misplaced Concreteness?," *International Journal of Systematic Theology* 5, no. 3 (November 2003): 287-308.

[67]Johannes Christiaan Hoekendijk, *The Church Inside Out* (New York: Westminster, 1966), 54.

[68]Kathryn Tanner, *Theories of Culture: A New Agenda for Theology* (Minneapolis: Fortress, 1997), 152.

[69]Newbigin, *Gospel in a Pluralist Society*, 227.

[70]Newbigin, "One Body," 153.

presence of the Spirit among [people]," is the "primary witness, anterior to all specific acts whether of service or preaching."[71] It is this kind of community that Newbigin has in mind when he calls the congregation the hermeneutic of the gospel.

The entire community participates as the hermeneutic of the gospel through both intentional and dimensional ways, supported by gifts of the Spirit that enliven and sustain the church in her calling to bear witness—the preeminent gift of the Spirit, and the one that properly orients all the others, is love.[72] What intellectual capacities, social skills, physical attributes, or sensory capacities does one need in order to love? Newbigin offers one vision of how people with disabilities participate in this community. In his short article he is making an explicit application of his belief, "Nothing will be consistent with the Gospel except a form of corporate Christian life which enables Christian love and concern to overleap every barrier of place, race, creed and party, and to express itself in relevant ways everywhere."[73] If this is truly the case, then our congregation and our witness are "not whole without [people with disabilities]."

AN EXAMPLE: "NOT WHOLE WITHOUT THE HANDICAPPED"

Beyond Amos Yong, I know of only one mission scholar who has addressed the issue of disability and witness directly: Lesslie Newbigin.[74] The stage was set for Newbigin's work by the Fifth Assembly of the WCC in Nairobi, 1975, and the "Report from Section II: What Unity Requires," which emphasized that visible church unity is essential to Christian witness. In the subheading "Unity Requires a Fuller Understanding of the Context," the document acknowledged that the context of the church increasingly includes people with disabilities: "Accidents and illness leave adults and children disabled; many more are emotionally handicapped by the pressures of social change and urban living; genetic disorders and famine leave millions of

---

[71]Ibid., 153-54.

[72]See Michael Barram, "'Fools for the Sake of Christ': Missional Hermeneutics and Praxis in the Corinthian Correspondence," *Missiology* 42, no. 2 (2015): 195-207, for an exposition of Paul's rhetoric of mission where that which is considered weak is indispensable.

[73]Newbigin, "One Body," 156.

[74]I also address disability and witness in my *Amplifying Our Witness: Giving Voice to Adolescents with Developmental Disabilities* (Grand Rapids: Eerdmans, 2012).

children physically or mentally impaired."[75] While the understanding of
disability represented at Nairobi is a deficient understanding of disability in
terms of illness or impairment, there is a missiology at work within the
WCC more along the lines of the Faith and Order movement, which emphasizes the necessity of the visible unity of the church for the sake of faithful
Christian witness. Despite being hampered by an operative medical model
of disability, the statement does make an early contribution to a missiological interpretation of disability:

> The Church cannot exemplify "the full humanity revealed in Christ," bear
> witness to the interdependence of humankind, or achieve unity in diversity if
> it continues to acquiesce in the social isolation of disabled persons and to
> deny them full participation in its life. The unity of the family of God is hand-
> icapped where these brother and sisters are treated as objects of conde-
> scending charity. It is broken where they are left out. . . . How can the Church
> be open to the witness which Christ extends through them?[76]

The missiological turn helped the framers of the report break with societal
norms and challenge the church to consider potential gains to the congregation's witness if the life and voice of people with disabilities are included. A
more theologically robust example of a missiological approach to disability
was offered a few years later by Newbigin.

In "Not Whole Without the Handicapped," Lesslie Newbigin offers a missiological perspective on including people with disabilities in the witness of
our congregations that can be critically appropriated today in light of the
missiological concepts I have explained above. I say *critically* appropriated
because on the one hand Newbigin inadvertently reinforces some of the
negative images and evaluations of people with disabilities through some
unfortunate articulations: he suggests that people "suffer from" "handicaps,"
which are primarily understood in terms of "deprivations"; he employs the
language of the courageous example who endures trials and overcomes obstacles. (The text is from the late 1970s.)

On the other hand, Newbigin offers some important insights about in-
clusiveness that can contribute to a more complete vision of the body of

---

[75]Michael Kinnamon and Brian E. Cope, eds., *The Ecumenical Movement: An Anthology of Key
Texts and Voices* (Grand Rapids: Eerdmans, 1997), 111-12.
[76]Ibid.

Christ and a more faithful witness. He challenges the notion that we live in a world without limits and encourages the church to embrace these limitations and incorporate them into her witness. He also identifies people with disabilities as among the oppressed and suggests that they are "utterly indispensable to the Church's authentic life," and he characterizes people with disabilities not as "a problem to be solved" but as "trustees of a blessing without which the Church cannot bless the world."[77]

While Newbigin never makes the connection directly, what he is doing in "Not Whole Without the Handicapped" is making the same missiological argument for including people with disabilities in the church's witness that he has made many times and in many other places for the necessity of the cultural pluriformity of the Church's witness.

His basic argument pivots off the orienting phrase "The saving power of God is to be carried and communicated by those who have no power to save themselves."[78] He highlights this paradox in the life and mission of Jesus, his disciples, and finally the church, concluding, "The strange truth about the Church is that when it can claim to be strong it is weak, and when it shares in the weakness of Christ it is truly the bearer of the power of God for the salvation of men and women everywhere."[79] Unfortunately, his understanding is that people with disabilities have an essential role in the community because they remind the community of its own insufficiency; the presence of people with disabilities reminds the community not to seek to be "healthy, strong, and free from all defects."[80] They (those with disabilities) remind us (presumably those without disabilities) of the truth of the paradox of strength in weakness and the hope that what is now hidden will be made manifest. The church is both the "society that fights and rebels" (represented by able-bodiedness in this discourse) and the "society that preaches resignation, that seeks to comfort the sufferer so that affliction becomes bearable" (a concern represented by disability in the midst of the

---

[77]J. E. Lesslie Newbigin, "Not Whole Without the Handicapped," in *Partners in Life: The Handicapped and the Church*, ed. Geiko Müller-Fahrenholz (Geneva: WCC Publications, 1979), 24-25. Newbigin obviously uses the language of the time to speak about intellectual disability. Years from now, I imagine the language I am using in this text will be dated.

[78]Ibid., 18.

[79]Ibid.

[80]Ibid., 20.

church).[81] People with disabilities are presented as being indispensable because of the lessons *they* teach *us*. People with disabilities teach the church how to be courageous in the face of difficult obstacles and how to be faithful in accepting limits. In summary, "They are the bearers of a witness without which the strong are lost in their own illusions," and "their presence in the church is the indispensable corrective of our inveterate tendency to identify the power of God with our power."[82]

If I have clearly articulated my argument to this point in the book, readers will not be surprised to find that I find Newbigin's engagement with disability less than adequate. At the same time, I have much hope in my disability imagination and in fact have offered a favorable representation of his work from the standpoint of his missiology elsewhere.[83] What Newbigin could have done, and what I intend to do in the rest of this chapter, is make the a missiological argument for including people with disabilities in the church's witness using Newbigin's insights about the necessity of the cultural pluriformity of the church's witness.

One of the most hopeful insights in Newbigin's article is underdeveloped. His understanding of the congregation as the "hermeneutic of the gospel" informs his argument but isn't articulated. While he doesn't use this terminology in this article, he is saying that the community won't represent the fullness of humanity or the way of Christ properly without including people with disabilities. In order to really be the hermeneutic of the gospel, the Christian community must include the way of strength in weakness and not hide weaknesses. The unfortunate byproduct of his argument is that people with disabilities are presented only as representing the weakness of the congregation. In what John Flett explains as the "double character" of the church—the "dialectic of cross and resurrection," the "church's special visibility," or the life of the congregation between the crucifixion and resurrection—the disabled serve to represent the fact that the church is "marked by suffering,"[84] but they also serve to "expose the false claims made by the principalities and

---

[81]Ibid., 23.

[82]Ibid., 25.

[83]Benjamin T. Conner, "Enabling Witness: Disability in Missiological Perspective," *Journal of Disability and Religion* 19, no. 1 (2015): 15-29. In this article I interpret Newbigin to be doing what I wished he had done.

[84]Newbigin, *Gospel in a Pluralist Society*, 107.

powers" as "part of its missionary witness."[85] Pushing against the tendency to seek power as the way to bear witness in the world is certainly an important role for people with disabilities in our congregations. But this is an incomplete perspective and certainly not the only or primary contribution that people with disabilities make to their congregations. People with disabilities also participate as Spirit-enabled "signs of the kingdom, powers of healing and blessing which, to eyes of faith, are recognizable as true signs that Jesus reigns."[86]

The presence of people with disabilities using their gifts in the service of the kingdom of God presents a challenge to the powers of the world. What the church needs in order to have a more credible witness in the world is not a separate program for people with disabilities (though such a program is at times beneficial) but the presence of people with disabilities as full members of the community. In Newbigin's terms, "The communication gap between the Gospel and the world is not bridged by a programme of contextualization—necessary as that is. It is bridged by an action of the Holy Spirit using the faithfulness of those who God has called into the life in Christ."[87] Such communication involves the "whole body of believers" as the "instrument of contextualization for the Gospel."[88]

Since missiology addresses a universal concern (the gospel) in a way that is local and contextual, it is a field of study that accentuates the cultural pluriformity of the gospel. As Newbigin has explained elsewhere, "As the mission goes its way to the ends of the earth new treasures are brought into the life of the Church and Christianity itself grows and changes until it becomes more credible as a foretaste of the unity of all humankind."[89] In Newbigin's theology of mission, *The Open Secret*, he adds the following: "The living Holy Spirit takes all that the Father has given to humankind—all people of every creed and culture—and declares it to the church as that which belongs to Christ as Lord. In this encounter the Church is changed,

---

[85]John G. Flett, "What Does It Mean for a Congregation to Be a Hermeneutic?," in *The Gospel and Pluralism Today: Reassessing Lesslie Newbigin in the 21st Century*, ed. Scott W. Sunquist and Amos Yong (Downers Grove, IL: IVP Academic, 2015), 204-5.

[86]Newbigin, *Gospel in a Pluralist Society*, 108.

[87]J. E. Lesslie Newbigin, "Context and Conversion," *International Review of Mission* 68, no. 270 (April 1979): 312.

[88]Ibid.

[89]Newbigin, *Gospel in a Pluralist Society*, 123-24.

the world is changed, and Christ is glorified."[90] Newbigin's insights apply equally to the impact that including people with disabilities in our congregational life can have on our doctrine and witness, as he has claimed in the contribution under consideration. Although he seems to overemphasize the courage of the disabled and their example of accepting limits, Newbigin continues, helpfully,

> Without that witness from within its own membership, the Church's witness is distorted and deceptive, and the Church's discipleship is irrelevant to the real world in which men and women live and suffer. For it is only when the witness of the handicapped is an integral part of the witness of the whole Church, that this witness is true to the Gospel of the Crucified who is risen, the risen Lord who is the Crucified. Only with this witness as part of its total message does the Church's message measure up to the heights and depths of the human situation.[91]

In this missiological way of thinking, people with disabilities are understood to be an essential part of the diversity of the human experience and necessary contributors to the calling of the church to bear witness to the ongoing redemptive work of God in this world by proclaiming the kingdom of God is at hand. As members of the body of Christ, they participate in this proclamation as sign, instrument, and foretaste of that kingdom. Newbigin asks, "Do we recognize in them members in the Body of Christ without whose gift we are maimed?"[92] Or, put positively in line with the title of this book: Do we acknowledge that people with disabilities are members of the body of Christ who enable a more credible witness in a world of people with differing abilities?

---

[90]Newbigin, *Open Secret*, 182-83.
[91]Newbigin, "Not Whole Without the Handicapped," 24.
[92]Ibid., 19.

PART II

Toward Enabling Witness

The next three chapters offer examples of enabling witness through [dis]abling mission studies and theological education. Phrases such as "deaf to the ways of God," "blind to the truth," or even Andrew Walls's phrase from the last chapter, "disabled from bringing Christ to bear," cast disabilities as inabilities and perpetuate within the church and graduate theological institutions a negative orientation toward persons with disabilities. The following chapters attempt to [dis]able our mission history, theology of witness, and theological education by considering the gifts and possibilities people with disabilities bring to our practice of witness, evangelism, and congregational life.

In "Teaching Theology from an Intercultural Perspective," Robert Schreiter summarizes the dynamics of interaction between power and difference across cultures in the following terms: *homogenizing, colonizing, demonizing, romanticizing,* and *pluralizing.*[1] These dynamics can also be used to describe

---

[1]Robert J. Schreiter, "Teaching Theology from an Intercultural Perspective," *Theological Education* 26, no. 1 (1989): 13-34.

the way Christians have engaged disability in mission history, theology of witness, and in our graduate theological institutions—a kind of crosscultural interaction where power dynamics are at play to the disadvantage of people with disabilities. Enabling witness requires addressing these issues and [dis] abling our approach to dealing with differences.

To expand Schreiter's concepts to apply to people with disabilities, to homogenize people with disabilities is to assume "*they* are all the same." But, as Dr. Stephen Shore, author, musician, artist, and autism self-advocate has pithily stated, "If you've met one person with autism, you've met one person with autism."[2] Of course, such heterogeneity applies to all people with disabilities. While people with disabilities may have common experiences of oppression or share similar traits or physical manifestations related to a disability, each person comes with his or her own unique gifts and limitations. To colonize people with disabilities is to use power to control them. As we saw in chapter one, Liat Ben-Moshe has clearly demonstrated how people with disabilities have been "incarcerated" in many forms in the United States. To demonize people with disabilities is to suggest that their differences have either a demonic or fundamentally "fallen" origin. Sadly, as we will examine in chapter three, throughout history normate interpretations of Scripture and uncritically accepted American values have been used to demonize d/Deaf people.

Romanticizing people with disabilities reduces them to virtuous suffers, inspirational examples, and holy innocents. There are many other concepts by which people with disabilities are flattened and appropriated for the benefit of those considered able-bodied. Pluralizing moves beyond homogenizing; it suggests beyond "they are all the same" that "we are all the same"—or in this case, "we are all disabled." Though the sentiment might be sincere, the reality is that there are significant differences in how people with disabilities experience the world related to their impairments that simply cannot be glossed over with such phrases. Schreiter explains that seminaries need to avoid these control mechanisms, but argues further, "It seems that the only way to accept the other as other is to admit the possibility of change on the part of the self. If that is ruled out, some

---

[2] "94 Favorite Quotes About Autism and Aspergers," The Art of Autism, February 1, 2018, the-art-of-autism.com/favorite-quotes-about-autism-and-aspergers/.

form of domination utilizing these five dynamics will be in play."[3] Chapter five will address these concerns directly. The call to [dis]able theology and missiology is a call to change the way we engage people whom we perceive as different or the other.

---

[3]Schreiter, "Teaching Theology from an Intercultural Perspective," 19.

3

······································

"Deaf to the Ways of God"

I had an interesting conversation with a Deaf friend recently. We were imagining what life will be like in glory and trying to theologically navigate the space between the position of Nancy Eiesland, who imagines that her heavenly body will still include her familiar power chair and braces, and that of my friend Randy, who hopes his future doesn't include his chair. When the discussion turned to deafness, my friend communicated to me, "I may be able to hear in heaven, but you will certainly be Deaf." By this he meant there is an embodied and relational element to Deaf communication that he wishes for me to experience as much as I wish him to hear the chirping of birds, rustling of reeds, or the words of the psalms. He hopes that I, though hearing, can be Deaf to the ways of God in the world.

WHY BRING DEAFNESS AND DEAF CULTURE INTO THE CONVERSATION?

There are good reasons for me *not* to bring the concept and experience of deafness or the Deaf community into this discussion about the relationship between missiology and disability.[1] One reason is that I am not d/Deaf, so I lack the insider perspective that is necessary for true Deaf theologizing. Deaf theologians Hannah Lewis and Kirk VanGilder highlight the distinctive viewpoint gained by the Deaf ontological experience. They register unique perspectives on oppression, the emphasis on collective storytelling, and the

---

[1]You will notice many different designations: deaf, Deaf, d/Deaf. I will explain the difference more fully in the coming pages, but, briefly, *deaf* refers to a degree of hearing loss and to people who understand themselves to have hearing loss. *Deaf* refers to a people (and their culture) who have a strong deaf identity and don't understand themselves in terms of auditory impairment. *d/Deaf* refers to both groups.

importance of dialogical process in Deaf theologizing.[2] In fact, in her book *Deaf Liberation Theology*, Hannah Lewis emphasizes, "I am really not interested in what hearing people, however involved with Deaf people they might be, have said about what Deaf people think and what a theology of Deaf people might look like. This is intended to be a Deaf theology full of Deaf voices."[3]

I do not intend to construct a Deaf missiology. Instead, this chapter attempts to follow Deaf insights on theology and missiology by drawing on dialogues with Deaf theologians and ministers, privileging d/Deaf perspectives, and examining the history of mission and evangelism in the United

---

[2]Hannah Lewis and Kirk VanGilder, "A Dialogue on Deaf Theology: Deaf Ontologies Seeking Theology," in *Innovations in Deaf Studies: The Role of Deaf Scholars*, ed. Annelies Kusters, Maartje De Meulder, and Dai O'Brien (Oxford: Oxford University Press, 2017), 169-90.
[3]Hannah Lewis, *Deaf Liberation Theology* (Aldershot, UK: Ashgate, 2007), 6.

States to and with d/Deaf persons in order to think differently about mission, disability, and witness.[4] At the end of this chapter the reader will have had a positive interaction with the phrase "Deaf to the ways of God."

A second reason not to include the d/Deaf in this broader discussion of disability and missiology is that many Deaf people don't understand themselves to be disabled. My conversations with Deaf scholars have brought this point home forcefully. Kirk VanGilder, Deaf scholar and assistant professor of religion at Gallaudet University, explains, "The whole rejection of 'disability' is a shifting target culturally and somewhat generationally also as younger deaf who embrace intersectional models of identity are less prone to rejecting the disability label. The generation who came of age during the most recent birth of Deaf Studies may generally reject disability labels unless politically expedient to embrace (i.e. ADA protections and FCC regulations)."[5] Noah Buchholz responds,

> Everyone has a different idea about including Deaf culture in Disability Studies. I think it's very difficult to address this issue; this has always been a grey area in Deaf Studies. If possible, you might want to be more clear about your reason for including Deaf people in your book. Or, you could simply state something like, "It is important to note that many Deaf people do not consider themselves to be disabled," and leave it as it is and let people examine themselves why some people, including Deaf people themselves, include Deaf culture in Disability Studies. I think it is appropriate to include Deaf culture in Disability Studies because many issues in Disability Studies certainly apply to the Deaf cultural community. At the same time, we ought to be careful not to, to use your word, *homogenize* Deaf people with other people with disabilities, especially because discussions about Deaf people must also take in consideration cultural and linguistic issues, unlike discussions about other people with disabilities. This is the reason why we cannot rely on Disability Studies alone when discussing about Deaf people, we need a separate field, that is, Deaf Studies. For example, oftentimes, my colleagues

---

[4]Special thanks to Tom Hudspeth (executive pastor at Lovers Lane UMC and pastor of deaf ministries) and Chad Entinger (executive director of deaf missions), who offered themselves for interviews during the research phase of this chapter, and to Noah Buchholz (assistant professor of ASL and deaf studies at Bethel College) and Kirk VanGilder (assistant professor of religion at Gallaudet University), who also gave interviews as well as invaluable feedback as I drafted this chapter.

[5]Correspondence with Kirk VanGilder, February 14, 2017.

who have disabilities discuss about how churches need to include people with disabilities more. To the contrary, many Deaf theologians and ministry leaders discuss about how hearing churches need to let Deaf people go and let them to have their own church where they can worship through their own language and culture.[6]

Hence, those who self-identify as Deaf largely recognize themselves as a linguistic minority who are more visually and kinesthetically oriented than aurally or orally. In fact, some Deaf people consider hearing people disabled, as Harlan Lane explains: "Naturally enough, members of the Deaf-World in the U.S. frequently view hearing people, with their more limited capacities in visual perception and manual language, and their misbegotten attitudes toward visual people, as possessing some serious limitations."[7] So why would I include the Deaf community in this conversation on disability and missiology and risk limiting appreciation of the gifts and possibilities of the d/Deaf by employing the category of "disability"? Shouldn't I be concerned that by doing so I lend further support to a limiting misperception of Deaf persons that defines them primarily in terms of limitations?

There are, nonetheless, compelling reasons to include d/Deafness in this discussion of disability and missiology. The primary and most forceful rationale is the fact that it can be maintained that Deaf culture in the United States originated and developed from the context of the nineteenth-century missionary movement. Mission studies include mission history, and one cannot address mission and evangelism in the United States without considering the reality of deafness. As I will explain below, the desire to evangelize deaf people led to the establishment of residential schools and created among deaf people an intergenerational community that valued and perpetuated the language and dispositions that became foundational to Deaf culture.

Another reason that mission studies should engage d/Deafness and Deaf culture is that reimagining Deaf in terms of "Deaf gain" rather than hearing loss enriches our theology and our practice of the faith, including our practices of mission and evangelism. Deafness is one variation of human existence

---

[6]Email correspondence with Noah Buchholz, February 12, 2017.
[7]Harlan Lane, Robert Hoffmeister, and Ben Bahan, *A Journey into the Deaf-World* (San Diego: Dawn Sign, 1996), 408.

that is a potential source for theological insight. Evangelism in the United States has a history of depending on an overly rational, logocentric approach to Christianity. Missiological engagement with the Deaf community shows us ways we have compromised the heart of Christianity (the embodied communication of love), diminished the importance of bodies and the senses, and overemphasized rationality.

Furthermore, missiology is always crossing boundaries in order to grasp a fuller understanding and experience of the reality of God at work in the world. Recognizing all the time that as a hearing person I am a limited and thus a disabled interloper in the Deaf world, in my missiological exploration I have committed to dialogue with Deaf partners as an acknowledgment of the importance of contextualization and as a demonstration of my respect for a Deaf way of theologizing. Indeed, my greatest insights are going to develop out of dialogue with Deaf partners.

Finally, there are issues related to evangelistic strategy and method, and issues of righteousness and justice with respect to our d/Deaf sisters and brothers, that the church needs to recognize and address if it is to remain faithful to its mission.

Notice the two different spellings of d/Deaf. d/Deaf people, as we have observed about all groupings of persons with disabilities, are not a homogeneous group. There are those who, having lost a degree of hearing later in life, feel that being deaf is a disabling condition. Some people are deaf from birth and born into Deaf families, learning sign language and Deaf cultural values from birth. More often than not (over 90 percent of the time), deaf children are born to hearing parents and are not introduced to sign language unless their parents choose to learn it or until they attend a Deaf school, where they learn sign language and about Deaf culture at the same time. Some d/Deaf people are deafened postlingually through accident or disease. Many such persons consider themselves "hard of hearing," and some can communicate effortlessly in the language of the majority culture (which, to this point in history, is spoken and written English).

Advocacy groups exist for every imaginable d/Deaf group. Considering the vision and goals of these advocacy groups can yield insight into the different ways that people connect to deafness or Deaf culture and to the kinds of issues that are important across the spectrum of d/Deaf. For example, a

group for children of deaf adults, CODA International (Coda-International
.org), celebrates and supports the multicultural identity of *hearing* children
who were raised in a Deaf culture communicating through sign language.
In this case there is a close identification with Deaf culture by hearing people.
Many of the organizations or associations oriented toward hearing loss
(rather than Deaf cultural identity) offer information and support related to
the use of technology, lip/speech reading, written and spoken language,
cochlear implants, and other assistive and medical technologies. The primary
support and advocacy organization for the Deaf, National Association of the
Deaf (NAD.org), on the other hand, focuses on the civil rights of the Deaf
person, training in American Sign Language (ASL), advocacy, litigation,
and education in support of the Deaf person as Deaf.

The differences between these organizations is exemplified in the recent
controversy between Nyle DiMarco—a Deaf model, contestant on *Dancing
with the Stars,* and advocate of ASL—and the A. G. Bell Association for the
Deaf and Hard of Hearing, which sees ASL as diminishing in value in the
face of technological advances. DiMarco wants at least bicultural education
for young deaf children (English and ASL) due to deleterious impact of
delays in language acquisition when only oral approaches or assistive technology are used.[8] He argues that an increase in ASL vocabulary corresponds with increases in English vocabulary, that learning ASL does not
interfere with a child learning to speak, and further that "early sign language
input can compensate for the lack of early auditory input."[9] In opposition
to DiMarco, the A. G. Bell Association noted that since over 90 percent of
deaf children are born to hearing adults, and since 90 percent of the families
of these children are choosing oral/aural language skills with assisting technology, Deaf culture and sign language are becoming less significant for the
identity of deaf persons and are no longer the primary means of communication for the deaf. DiMarco is, according to A. G. Bell's logic, offering mis-
leading information about a limited understanding of deafness and risks

---

[8]Sarah Polus, "A 'Dancing with the Stars' Contestant Is Vying for a White House Correspondents'
    Dinner Invite," *Washington Post,* March 28, 2016, www.washingtonpost.com/news/reliable
    -source-wp/2016/03/28/a-dancing-with-the-stars-contestant-is-vying-for-a-white-house
    -correspondents-dinner-invite/.
[9]"Welcome to Parents' Corner," Nyle DiMarco Foundation, accessed March 11, 2018, nyledimarco
    foundation.com/parents-corner/.

putting children at a disadvantage in society by pushing for sign language.[10] Whereas the Deaf community understands A. G. Bell to be continuing their namesake's mission to destroy Deaf culture while embracing an exclusively narrow conception of language that is restricted to speaking and listening, the supporters of A. G. Bell's position—many of them deaf and hard-of-hearing people who are thriving or are at ease in the hearing world—feel that the conception of Deaf promoted by DiMarco and others is unnecessarily restrictive and needs to be broadened to include them.

As you can see, the issues of d/Deaf and able/disabled are complex. This chapter will contribute to the larger themes of this book by introducing the reader to the creation of Deaf people as a disabled group by an ableist (in this case audist) culture. At the same time I will demonstrate how missionary impulses contributed positively to Deaf identity and culture in a liberating way while further exacerbating cultural fears and misperceptions of difference. Then I will describe how Deaf culture further complicates conceptions of ability and disability by considering how (largely successful) legislation intended to overcome the warehousing and abuse of people with disabilities has created what some have termed a "Deaf diaspora"—a complicating factor in perpetuating Deaf culture that has created a missiological challenge for those invested in ministry to and with the Deaf. Finally, I will use missiological categories to imagine ways in which "Deaf gain" can amplify the witness of the church, and I will identify ongoing discrimination against and exclusion of the Deaf that need to be addressed by missiologists and congregations in the name of justice and peace, which is a part of God's redemptive work in the world.

THE CULTURAL CONSTRUCTION OF D/DEAF PEOPLE AS DISABLED

The cultural construction of d/Deaf people as disabled and the identification of deaf people as a focused target of Christian evangelism in the United States developed simultaneously in a particular social and economic environment, an atmosphere that also had implications for nineteenth-century understandings of mission. An American society that had been created around communal identities was fading, and a new understanding

---

[10]Meredith Sugar, "Dispelling Myths About Deafness," AG Bell, April 1, 2016, www.agbell.org/in-the-news/response-nyle-dimarco (since removed from website).

of the individual in relationship to productive capacities was emerging. The industrial revolution was marginalizing people who were different from what was coming to be measured, classified, and standardized as the normal or average worker. The sweep of cultural change was stimulated by immigration, urbanization, and increased mobility, and together these factors stimulated fearful feelings of societal dissolution and personal uncertainty. Under such conditions, one way stability was achieved in society was by elevating the notions of conformity and sameness and imagining nearly interchangeable "productive citizens" who could contribute to the creation of a better America. Those who didn't fit the standards were further marginalized as machines, buildings, and transportation structures necessary for thriving in such a society were oriented toward able-bodied, sighted, and hearing persons.

Jan Branson and Don Miller contend that as mechanistic science became the religion of Western culture, providing both the epistemological and cosmological framework for society, spirituality became increasingly individualized and intellectualized. That which had previously been viewed as simply part of human diversity now threatened order and was instead defined in terms of anomaly or pathology, thus creating a class of persons, "the disabled." The drive to classify, measure, and document led to the marginalization of people whose bodies or minds appeared beyond the norms, especially those who weren't seen as having the intellectual capacity to distinguish them from animals. As Branson and Miller write, "The eventual marginalization of certain human difference by labeling them as pathological and, thus, as less than or other than human was directly tied to the marginalization of other nonhuman beings. As zoos developed, so too did the display of human 'others' in fairs, marketplaces, and hospitals for the insane such as Bedlam."[11]

As advances in transportation, communication, industry, innovations in education, and emerging urban centers brought people together, deaf people had the benefit of getting to know other deaf people who shared similar experiences but also had the misfortune of being constructed by hearing society as disabled and experiencing oppression as a group. Deaf people

---

[11]Jan Branson and Don Miller, *Damned for Their Difference: The Cultural Construction of Deaf People as Disabled* (Washington, DC: Gallaudet University Press, 2002), 23.

were being defined as a homogenous, pathological, and unproductive group, and the deaf person was understood by the public to be something other than a citizen. Leonard Davis in explaining the phenomenon explicitly says, "The disabled person is not of this nation, is not a citizen, in the same sense as the able-bodied."[12] Branson and Miller further clarify, "Although most had experienced the hardships of individual discrimination before, they were now to experience a shared discrimination, being discriminated against as a category of humanity, as 'deaf' and 'disabled.'"[13]

Additionally, in the late nineteenth century the eugenics movement amplified the impact of ethnocentric nationalism and confronted people viewed as disabled with the possibility of elimination. Eugenics was conceived by Sir Francis Galton (Charles Darwin's cousin), and eugenicists promoted "a concept of beauty that was white and able-bodied while often portraying the undesirable 'disabled' as non-whites."[14] Pathological differences, like congenital deafness, were viewed negatively and, "especially when that pathology was present from birth, became akin to the otherness of another race or even another species."[15] Such thinking was pervasive and found support in some surprising advocates.

What comes to mind when you consider the name "Alexander Graham Bell"? Do you think of the scientist and inventor who invented the telephone? If you were Deaf, you might have a different perspective. Your muscles might tighten as you consider the one who stated that deaf people reproducing would issue in "the production of a defective race of human beings," people whose existence would be "a great calamity to the world."[16]

In a paper he presented to the National Academy of Science at New Haven in 1883, Bell suggested how such a defective race might come to be, touching on the significant contributions of the Deaf schools in creating social networks and a sense of connection among Deaf people and recasting those benefits as liabilities. If you wanted to create a defective race

---

[12]Lennard J. Davis, *Enforcing Normalcy: Disability, Deafness, and the Body* (New York: Verso, 1995), 91.
[13]Branson and Miller, *Damned for Their Difference*, 139.
[14]Ibid., 30. The term *eugenics* is derived from the Greek *eugenes*, which means "good birth."
[15]Ibid., 31.
[16]Alexander Graham Bell, "Memoir upon the Formation of a Deaf Variety of the Human Race: A Paper Presented to the National Academy of Science at New Haven," November 13, 1883, archive.org/stream/gu_memoirformatioobell#page/n7/mode/2up, 41.

of people, he claimed, you would place them together from a young age, promote social interaction among them, offer religious and state support to them, support the development of Deaf societies, develop a national organization to support them, make sure they have newspapers and periodicals that address their concerns and interests, and, most powerfully, "teach the deaf-mutes to think in a different language from the people at large."[17] Despite the fact that his mother was deaf, the "deaf-mute," in the mind of Bell, would always remain a foreigner. Consequently, Bell wished to discourage marriage among Deaf people, shut down Deaf schools, and "cure" the world of deafness.

Bell did note that many deaf-mutes face prejudice from hearing persons, a fact he seemed to lament. However, his sympathy did not override his desire to address the perceived defect—the lack of hearing or the consequential "formation of a deaf variety of the human race," which he found to be counterproductive to a healthy and unified society. Therefore, he proposed both repressive and preventative measures to deter the tendency of deaf people to breed other deaf people. His most damaging proposal was that deaf persons not be segregated into residential schools for the deaf: "The segregation of deaf-mutes, the use of the sign-language, and the employment of deaf teachers produce an environment that is unfavorable to the cultivation of articulation and speech-reading."[18] This was a proposition that was intended to transform the social environment of the deaf person and would slow or stop the evolution and use of sign language.

Life for many deaf people in the nineteenth century was a challenging experience fraught with experiences of discrimination and the loneliness of isolation. The great century of missionary expansion addressed these issues, though one could argue unintentionally, by creating an environment where deaf individuals would become Deaf people (a distinct people with a history, language, and culture), for instance, through the founding of evangelistic residential schools and recognizing sign language as the natural language of the deaf.

---

[17]Ibid., 42.
[18]Ibid., 48.

The Nineteenth-Century Mission Movement, Evangelism, and the Rise of Deaf Culture

The nineteenth century was fertile soil for the growth of reform movements and benevolent societies, concrete institutional outworkings of the Second Great Awakening and instruments of an incipient American version of evangelism that would fight to eradicate social ills. The religious response of disinterested benevolence, the development of asylums, and the urban missionary movement were animated by the emergence of a flexible and mobile innovation—the volunteer movement—fortified with paternalism, and primarily focused on reform in America.[19] As historian William Hutchinson clearly explains, "The confidence about reforming Europe and saving the world, so evident in the formal and popular expression of the revolutionary period, gave way to zeal for nation-building; the expansionism promoted as our 'manifest destiny' tended to be continental, not worldwide."[20]

Not only was mission in the United States self-oriented, but the vision of many missionaries was often driven by millennial hopes in a way that conflated nationalist and religious motivations such that "Christian obligation and American obligation were fundamentally harmonious."[21] Mission included both evangelism, reaching the "heathen" with the message of the gospel, and moral uplift, improving the world in preparation for Christ's millennial reign in tangible, concrete, and calculable ways. When it came to the relationship between the deaf and mission, both aspects of mission were motivating factors, and both can be seen clearly in the life and ministry of Thomas Hopkins Gallaudet, the founder of the evangelistic Connecticut Asylum for the Education and Instruction of Deaf and Dumb Persons.

Gallaudet, a graduate of Andover Theological Seminary who would eventually become a Congregational minister, was living in Hartford when he received his vocational identity of missionary educator to the deaf. The desire to teach his neighbor's deaf daughter, Alice Cogswell, ultimately led

---

[19]Sydney E. Ahlstrom, *A Religious History of the American People* (New Haven, CT: Yale University Press, 1972), 422. See also Daniel Walker Howe, *What God Hath Wrought: The Transformation of America, 1815–1848* (Oxford: Oxford University Press, 1997), chap. 5. Thanks to David Komline for the suggestion.

[20]William R. Hutchison, *Errand to the World: American Protestant Thought and Foreign Mission* (Chicago: University of Chicago Press, 1987), 43.

[21]Ibid., 44.

him—along with Alice's father, surgeon Mason Cogswell; and Laurent Clerc, the "apostle of the deaf people in the new world,"[22] a deaf Frenchman who was an expert in sign language—to open the Asylum (later renamed the American School for the Deaf).[23]

In terms of his theological understanding of mission, Gallaudet was a product of his time. At this point in history mission theology was anemic, and pragmatism and technique ruled the day. An implicit, functional missionary theology can be discerned, however, by examining Gallaudet's sermons and speeches. When we do so, we find that Gallaudet was evangelistic, was impacted by the revivals associated with the Awakening, and desired that all people have the chance to hear and respond to the message of the gospel of Jesus Christ. He was theologically trained at Andover, a school that was invested in mission and evangelism, and, Fernandes contends, he was guided by a millennial vision that pervaded the campus in the nineteenth century.[24] Consequently, Gallaudet regarded benevolent acts and fulfilling the missionary obligation as hastening the return of Christ and his blissful reign. He was also a product of his time in that he did not distinguish between citizenship and discipleship, although he did emphasize a conviction that there is no possibility of developing a healthy civic body without conversion to Christ.

Having gone through many of Gallaudet's speeches and sermons that illuminate his understanding of mission and communicate his purpose of establishing the Hartford Asylum, I will demonstrate how Gallaudet roots his conception of mission generally, and his mission to the deaf specifically, in his evangelistic mission theology. I will be joined in my analysis by the research of two rhetoricians who have analyzed Gallaudet's speeches and sermons for other reasons, but whose findings are particularly germane to my line of inquiry. Finally, I will suggest that despite being a creature of his time, Gallaudet had progressive views about the capacity of sign language to communicate effectively and was early to recognize it as the heart language of deaf people.

---

[22]See Loida R. Canlas, "Laurent Clerc: Apostle to the Deaf People of the New World," Laurent Clerc National Deaf Education Center, www3.gallaudet.edu/clerc-center/info-to-go/deaf-culture/laurent-clerc.html

[23]John Vickrey Van Cleve and Barry A. Crouch, *A Place of Their Own: Creating the Deaf Community in America* (Washington, DC: Gallaudet University Press, 1988), 32-41.

[24]James John Fernandes, "The Gate to Heaven: T. H. Gallaudet and the Rhetoric of the Deaf Education Movement" (PhD diss., University of Michigan, 1979).

Gallaudet clearly articulates his conception of mission in an address given in 1819 at a prayer meeting in support of the American Board of Commissioners for Foreign Mission (ABCFM) in Hawaii, then the Sandwich Islands. Drawing on the recently rediscovered missionary text Matthew 28:18-20 (particularly the phrase "Go ye, therefore, and teach all nations"),[25] Gallaudet was compelled by an "obligation," "an imperious duty" grounded in the "explicit command" of Jesus to evangelistically educate the deaf. Our obligation as people whose ancestors were enlightened by the truth of the gospel, he argued, is to convey that knowledge to the heathen world. In this address, Gallaudet clearly casts his vision for Christian mission and evangelistic proclamation as having a civilizing function, where civilization is understood in terms of his experience of society in the United States. In his words, the object of mission is "to bear the message of a Saviour's love to thousands of immortal souls who have never yet heard of him, and who are plunged in the depths of the lowest sensuality and sin," *and also* "to introduce the arts and comforts of civilized society among a race of people, who . . . know little or nothing of those social, intellectual and moral enjoyments which we prize as among our highest privileges."[26]

Similar to other advocates of mission in the early nineteenth century, Gallaudet believed that "the civilization of these islanders cannot be effected without, at the same time christianizing them."[27] The character of a society, he explained, is made up of the character of its individual members. Therefore, the philanthropists' goal to civilize and give the islanders the benefits of Western society would fail unless those efforts were accompanied by a corresponding spiritual transformation that would squelch immorality, conceived by Gallaudet and his contemporaries in terms of nativist animal passions.

---

[25] It may seem odd to suggest that a text that seems so obviously motivating for mission today was *rediscovered* just prior to 1819. The fact is that most theologians and congregational leaders of the Reformation viewed the so-called Great Commission to be directed only to the apostles and not applicable to any contemporary missionary obligation. It was not until William Carey popularized the verse in 1792 that it became relevant as a command to go and evangelize the world through his influential *Enquiry* (Johannes Verkuyl, *Contemporary Missiology: An Introduction* [Grand Rapids: Eerdmans, 1978], 24). See also William Carey, *An Enquiry into the Obligations of Christians to Use Means for the Conversion of the Heathens* (London: Carey Wingate, 1792).

[26] Thomas H. Gallaudet, *An Address, Delivered at a Meeting for Prayer, with Reference to the Sandwich Mission, in the Brick Church in Hartford, October 1, 1819* (Hartford, CT: Lincoln and Stone, 1819), 8.

[27] Ibid.

Gallaudet was unable to participate in the foreign missionary movement that was being launched from bases in the United States, yet he still viewed his missionary calling in terms of the apostle Paul's: not preaching Christ where he has already been named but instead to the "heathen of our day."[28] Who were the heathen according to Gallaudet? As he explained in his sermon titled "On the Duty and Advantages of Affording Instruction to the Deaf and Dumb," they were the millions in Europe, Asia, Africa, and the Sandwich Islands who were "enveloped with the midnight gloom of ignorance and superstition."[29] The heathen were also those closer to home who were "without any correct knowledge of the God who made them."[30] But the special focus of Gallaudet was the "long-neglected heathen;—the poor Deaf and Dumb, whose sad necessities have been forgotten, while scarce a corner of the world has not been searched to find those who are yet ignorant of Jesus Christ."[31]

Why should the deaf be considered heathen? Not due to their vices and sins; in fact Gallaudet believed that deaf people had been providentially protected by "the restraining grace of God" from much of the evil of the world.[32] They were heathen because "without instruction, they must inevitably remain ignorant of the most simple truths, even of what is termed Natural Religion, and of all those doctrines of Revealed religion."[33] The deaf were heathen, the objects of mission work, viewed similarly to other foreign people as fundamentally abnormal. Branson and Miller explain, "Missioners and educators, often the same, reflected the moral therapy movement in their concern for uplifting deaf people spiritually and morally so they could take their places alongside the 'normal' members of society. Their confinement was a confinement oriented toward moral regeneration which include the normalizing process of education."[34]

Once educated and morally oriented, the deaf had the potential to become valuable and useful members of society instead of "a burden to family and

---

[28]Thomas H. Gallaudet, *A Sermon, On the Duty and Advantages of Affording Instruction to the Deaf and Dumb* (Portland, ME: A. Shirley, 1824), 6.
[29]Ibid., 7.
[30]Ibid., 8.
[31]Ibid.
[32]Ibid., 11.
[33]Ibid., 12.
[34]Branson and Miller, *Damned for Their Difference*, 131.

friends" or objects of pity.[35] In fact, to evangelize deaf people through the means of the educational asylum, Gallaudet contended, is to rescue otherwise intelligent and potentially spiritual people from "non-existence."[36]

Therefore, the particular form that Gallaudet's mission to the deaf would take was the educational asylum. As he explained in a sermon delivered at the opening of the Connecticut Asylum for the Education and Instruction of Deaf and Dumb Persons, without education the deaf wouldn't be able to account for the wonders around them—they wouldn't be able to read the book of creation, understand typical human interactions, or have an understanding of eternity. In Gallaudet's opinion, their minds had a sickness, and their intellects were in chains without access to religious education. Viewing deaf persons with the same paternalistic lenses he would later use to consider the Hawaiians, Gallaudet enthusiastically invited his hearers to "witness, for the first time in this western world, the affecting sight of a little group of fellow-sufferers assembling for instruction, who neither sex, nor age, nor distance, could prevent from hastening to embrace the first opportunity of aspiring to the privileges that we enjoy, as rational, social, and immortal beings."[37] What I am critiquing is Gallaudet's characterization of deaf people and the conflation of becoming a Christian with becoming a good, useful citizen. I am not challenging his understanding that deaf people, like all other people, share an underlying need for Christ in order to make sense of the wonder of God in this world. As he would explain later at the dedication of the Asylum, Gallaudet viewed the institution as "the gate to heaven" for the deaf, leading to more than simply "earthy advantages."[38] In his optimistic view, his evangelism was motivated by the belief that the world would become what it was meant to be when the principles of the gospel were made "the universal rule of thought and conduct."[39]

---

[35]Gallaudet, *Duty and Advantages*, 19.

[36]Ibid., 23.

[37]Thomas H. Gallaudet, "A Sermon, Delivered at the Opening of the Connecticut Asylum for the Education and Instruction of Deaf and Dumb Persons, April 20th, 1817," in *Tribute to Gallaudet: A Discourse in Commemoration of the Life, Character and Services of the Rev. Thomas H. Gallaudet*, ed. Henry Barnard (Hartford, CT: Brockett & Hutchinson, 1852), 172.

[38]Ibid., 178. For more on Gallaudet's notion that his asylum was a gate to heaven, see Fernandes, *Gate to Heaven*.

[39]Gallaudet, "Sermon, Delivered at the Opening," 168.

In Gallaudet's mind, deaf people were among the heathen, and their evangelization would provide them with moral uplift, making them better citizens—and, importantly, hasten the return of Christ. In a sermon delivered at the opening of the Asylum, Gallaudet refers to "the universal diffusion of the gospel in these *latter* ages of the church, and to its happy influence upon the hearts of all mankind" and, later in the sermon, his hope that the Asylum "may be made the instruments of advancing that happy period, when *the heathen shall be given to Christ for his inheritance, and the uttermost parts of the earth for his possession.*"[40] As one scholar explains it, "Using the imagery of heathenism, darkness and imprisonment to characterize scenic devils and arouse pity for the uneducated deaf, the vision also projected hope in the form of the movement's apostles and saviors who would release the deaf from the chains of ignorance and heathenism and by do doing help prepare the way for the coming of Christ."[41]

Positively, the sermon was delivered in Vermont, Maine, and New Hampshire during an excursion to raise funds for the Asylum and "to excite in the public mind a deeper interest than has hitherto been felt for the Deaf and Dumb."[42] Unfortunately, like other missionaries of his time, his paternalism and nationalism were incongruent with his liberating message. An example of his paternalism and objectification of the deaf person is evidenced in Gallaudet's understanding that his role was "to soothe the distresses and dispel the ignorance of the unfortunate objects of our regard; while we would unfold to them the wonders of that religion, in which we profess to believe, and set before them the love of that Saviour, on whom all our hopes rest; let us be grateful to God for the very superior advantages which *we* enjoy."[43] Fortunately, as we will explore below, the gospel and the process of cross-cultural transmission seem to have a momentum of their own, especially in the lives of the indigenous appropriators. However, before we get to the possibilities of Deaf gain in our theology of ministry and witness, we will explore how Gallaudet was in fact progressive in his understanding of sign

---

[40]Ibid., 168, 173; italics in original.

[41]Fernandes, *Gate to Heaven*, 161.

[42]Gallaudet, introduction to *Duty and Advantages*.

[43]Gallaudet, "Sermon, Delivered at the Opening," 173. See also his "Sermon on the Duty and Advantages," where he characterizes the deaf as "consumed by a torpid indolence, and vacuity of thought" (19).

language. Gallaudet had an appreciation of, and offered a theological apologetic for, the use of sign language that made an important contribution to what would become Deaf culture. Years later, it would spawn Deaf theology and ministry.

Romans 10:17 ("So then faith cometh by hearing, and hearing by the word of God" in the King James Version), a verse that has traditionally inspired evangelism and mission, has been described by Van Cleve and Crouch as "the most damaging blow to deaf people in the New Testament."[44] Traditionally, this verse has been interpreted by hearing people to mean that faith is impossible for deaf people due to their inability to hear the Word of God. But Gallaudet did not despair. He was inspired by a different verse from Romans—Romans 15:21: "But, as it is written, To whom he has not spoken of, they shall see; and they that have not heard shall understand (KJV)". Another verse that similarly inspired Gallaudet in his ministry to the deaf-mute came from Isaiah, "the evangelical prophet." He begins his sermon offered at the opening of the Asylum with Isaiah 35:5-6:

> Then the eyes of the blind shall be opened,
>   and the ears of the deaf unstopped;
> then the lame shall leap like a deer,
>   and the tongue of the speechless sing for joy.
> For waters shall break forth in the wilderness
>   and streams in the desert.

Motivated by this prophetic utterance about the promise of comprehensibility, Gallaudet viewed his Asylum as participating in the fulfillment of this verse with sign language as a direct instrument enabling the deaf to hear the Word of God. Or, as Tracy Ann Morse states, "For Gallaudet, the deaf community was a mission field and education through sign language was a method for proselytizing the deaf."[45]

SIGN LANGUAGE, IDENTITY, AND DEAF CULTURE

It is around the issue of sign language that Gallaudet created the space necessary for Deaf culture to develop and offered some tools for Deaf

---

[44]Van Cleve and Crouch, *Place of Their Own*, 4.
[45]Tracy Ann Morse, "Seeing Grace: Religious Rhetoric in the Deaf Community" (PhD diss., University of Arizona, 2005), 29.

theologizing. Morse proposes that Gallaudet's support of deaf students being educated in their native language (sign language) was directly related to his Protestant evangelical leanings.

> Gallaudet's education at Andover Theological Seminary stressed the importance of "spreading the gospel." For Gallaudet, the deaf were lost souls who needed to be taught the importance of the Bible and the gospel message of Christ's birth, death, and resurrection. Gallaudet wanted to convert deaf Americans through a common language of signs that they would learn at the first permanent school for the Deaf.[46]

As Morse suggests, Gallaudet did have an instrumental reason for advocating sign language as the language of instruction for deaf people. Gallaudet believed that teaching someone to lip read and articulate words was a painstaking and seldom-successful process. A common language was needed with which "the deaf-mute can intelligibly conduct his private devotions, and join in social religious exercises with his fellow pupils."[47]

Indeed, beyond its instrumental role in the evangelization of deaf people, Gallaudet imagined sign language as a fully sufficient communication mode for conveying all truth, as he explained in his sermon *Duty and Advantages*: "For it is a most singular trait of the language of gestures and signs, that it is sufficiently significant and copious to admit of an application event to the most abstract intellectual, moral, and religious truth."[48] Going further, Gallaudet took on Romans 10:17 ("Faith cometh by hearing") when he drove a wedge between comprehension and written communication and valorized aural/oral communication, even giving sign language the advantage: "There is no more intrinsic or necessary connexion between ideas of whatever kind, and audible or written language, than between the same ideas, and the language of signs and gestures; and that the latter has even one advantage over the former, inasmuch as it possesses a power of analogical and symbolical description which can never belong to any combination of purely arbitrary sounds and letters."[49] In the language of mission

---

[46]Ibid., 16-17.
[47]T. H. Gallaudet, "On the Natural Language of Signs; and Its Value and Uses in the Instruction of the Deaf and Dumb," in *Supplement to the American Annals of the Deaf and Dumb* (New York: New York Institution for the Deaf and Dumb, 1878), 1:85.
[48]Gallaudet, *Duty and Advantages*, 17.
[49]Ibid., 18.

scholar Lamin Sanneh, Gallaudet was relativizing spoken language and destigmatizing sign language.[50]

Gallaudet believed that sign language had the potential to cultivate the mind of the deaf person as well as provide the opportunity to explore principles of the education of youth more generally.[51] This view was in part related to conventional understandings of the deaf person as having an untarnished, primitive mind and in part related to Scottish commonsense philosophy, particularly Dugald Stewart's appropriation of Thomas Reid's view that spoken language evolved from a primitive "gestural" language that "proved that each individual has an inner life of thought and feeling which does not come first from reasoning, but is a response to innate first principles."[52] But his support of sign language was ultimately grounded in his religious beliefs. As described by a Gallaudet scholar, "Not only was sign language an instrument of evangelism, as a means of providing religious instruction to the deaf, but it could also serve all people as a way to reveal and communicate the presence of the eternal soul. The final justification for the use of sign language was a religious one, for it would advance the spiritual perfection of man, bring him closer to God."[53] Therefore, years later when oralist-manualist debates ensued over the appropriate way to educate deaf people, Gallaudet had established firm ground for defending sign language, if not in education at least in religion, and had secured a place for sign language in the deaf religious experience.

While a difference of opinion always separated those who favored teaching deaf people lip reading and speech (oralists) and those who favored sign language as the primary language of the deaf in education (manualists), the 1880 International Conference of Teachers of the Deaf in Milan complicated things for those who favored sign language. In the mid-nineteenth century, even when schools chose to adopt oralism, there was still a place for the heart language of deaf people. As Morse explains, "Strictly oral schools removed sign language all together or relegated its use to religious

---

[50]Lamin O. Sanneh, *Translating the Message: The Missionary Impact on Culture* (Maryknoll, NY: Orbis, 2001), 1.

[51]Gallaudet, "Sermon, Delivered at the Opening," 169.

[52]Phyllis Klein Valentine, "American Asylum for the Deaf: A First Experiment in Education, 1817–1880" (PhD diss., University of Connecticut, 1993), 77; see also 68-85. Thanks, again, to David Komline for the insight.

[53]Fernandes, *Gate to Heaven*, 195.

training and chapel services. On this point, Gallaudet found common ground with oralists—he indicated deaf students should continue to have religious training and chapel services in sign language regardless of the chosen method of instruction."[54] Sign language bore some kind of capacity for religious communication—especially for those for whom it was their native language. However, by the late nineteenth century the Milan Conference, at which all but one of the 164 participants gathered from Europe and the United States were hearing and the majority of the delegates were clergy,[55] determined that oralism, articulation, and lip reading were favorable educationally over sign language and finger spelling.[56] The conference concluded, "This Congress, considering the incontestable superiority of speech over signs (1) in restoring the deaf mute to society (2) and in giving him a more perfect knowledge of language, declares, that the oral method ought to be preferred to that of signs for the education and instruction of the deaf and dumb."[57] By 1920, a stunning 80 percent of deaf students were educated and communicated with their teachers and peers without the use of sign language as a consequence of the impact of Milan.[58]

At the heart of the oralist argument was the persistent notion that deafness is fundamentally a defect that disqualified deaf people from being contributing citizens. The point is that deaf persons wouldn't make good citizens because they were resistant to learning the language and accepting the culture of the general population. "To exercise intelligently the rights of citizenship, then they must be made people of our language."[59] The manualists (those who favored sign language) often argued along the lines of Protestant theology that the Bible and the gospel message needed to be made accessible to deaf persons through their native language or that sign language was an "original language of mankind" and was therefore a

---

[54]Morse, "Seeing Grace," 47.

[55]Paddy Ladd, *Understanding Deaf Culture: In Search of Deafhood* (Tonawanda, NY: Multilingual Matters, 2003), 123.

[56]Van Cleve and Crouch, *Place of Their Own*, 108-9.

[57]Joseph Claybaugh Gordon, *Notes and Observations upon the Education of the Deaf with a Revised Index to Education of Deaf Children* (Washington, DC: Volta Bureau, 1892), xxxv.

[58]From 1882 to 1919, the percentage of deaf students being taught *without signs* rose from 7.5 percent to 80 percent. See Kenneth Robert Olney, "Religion and the American Deaf Community: A Sociological Analysis of the Chicago Mission for the Deaf, 1890–1941" (PhD diss., University of Oregon, 1999), 173.

[59]Douglass Baynton, in Davis, *Enforcing Normalcy*, 229.

"language closer to God and nature than speech, uncorrupted and pure, more honest because more direct as a means of emotional expression."[60] The oralists, as Baynton explains, "were of a generation frightened by growing cultural and linguistic diversity and more immediately concerned with the national community than the Christian one. . . . They associated sign language not with God and nature nor with gentility but with 'inferior races' and 'lower animals.'"[61] Morse concludes similarly, "In America, late nineteenth-century arguments opposing sign language and viewing deafness as a deficit were grounded in a desire for a national identity recognized by spoken English, the theory of evolution, and scientific thinking—stark contrasts to the manualist's arguments grounded in Protestant theology."[62]

The fight for sign language was a fight for the identity of the emerging Deaf community.

> In fighting for the spread of the manual method, teachers, both hearing and deaf, knew that they were contributing to the creation of a new community on the American scene, a Deaf community. It was a world that Deaf people would, of course, develop further after they graduated. But it was a world with its roots firmly planted in the residential schools. The residential schools were quintessentially Deaf places, even if staffed with significant numbers of hearing people.[63]

What ultimately preserved sign language, and consequently Deaf culture, was the fact that even when a school was an oral school, students still communicated in sign language in the halls and especially in religious spaces. Chapel services and sanctuaries became Deaf spaces where the use of sign language flourished even in the midst of debates between oralists and manualists.[64] Even when in the residential schools deaf teachers were demoted and sign language was banned in the classroom, the religious services provided a place where students could use sign language and connect with deaf leaders and role models who would address students in sign language. Sign

---

[60]Douglas C. Baynton, *Forbidden Signs: American Culture and the Campaign Against Sign Language* (Chicago: University of Chicago Press, 1996), 9.

[61]Ibid., 16.

[62]Morse, "Seeing Grace," 47.

[63]R. A. R. Edwards, *Words Made Flesh: Nineteenth-Century Deaf Education and the Growth of Deaf Culture* (New York: New York University Press, 2012), 28-29.

[64]Morse, "Seeing Grace," 18.

language was able to retain this position in the schools even after 1900, when most residential schools for deaf students were dominated by oralism.[65] To go a step further, Morse reasons, "The sanctuary Protestant churches provided deaf adults in the late nineteenth and early twentieth-century America by ministering to them in sign language was significant to the stabilization of an emerging deaf community recognized by its use of sign language."[66] Even in schools established by the state and without the explicit evangelistic mandate of Gallaudet's Asylum, chapel services preserved sign language and a Deaf religious identity. Otto Berg thus notes, "Even in the residential schools that were created later by legislative action, Christian mores and morality were given an import place. For instance, most State schools required the children enrolled to attend daily chapel exercises, and on Sundays there was Sunday school for all."[67]

What the schools really accomplished, beyond the evangelistic efforts and training for trades, was allowing the space necessary for the development of a Deaf culture. Before Gallaudet and the residential schools, there was no Deaf culture; there were only deaf individuals scattered across the face of the country. They couldn't organize themselves because they were isolated from each other and did not have a shared language. Education motivated by mission and evangelism brought deaf persons together, supported the establishment of a shared language, and consequently was the handmaiden to Deaf culture.

The Deaf schools created Deaf culture because deaf Americans began to socialize, develop relationships, form clubs, and upon graduation seek the same kind of fellowship they had experienced at the school. Those who had been scattered could now form community around a common language and some common experiences. "As students went on to graduate and leave schools, they often found themselves in communities with very few other

---

[65]"By 1900, nearly all the schools [residential schools for deaf students] had a strong oral emphasis, and many prohibited signing among their students. Yet when Hasenstab visited and addressed the students, he delivered his messages in sign language. Religious services provided rare opportunities when signing was still allowed at many deaf schools." Kent R. Olney, "The Chicago Mission for the Deaf," in *The Deaf History Reader*, ed. John Vickrey Van Cleve (Washington, DC: Gallaudet University Press, 2007), 198.

[66]Morse, "Seeing Grace," 86.

[67]Otto B. Berg, *A Missionary Chronicle: Being a History of the Ministry to the Deaf in the Episcopal Church, 1850–1980* (Winona, MN: St. Mary's Press, 1984), xiv.

deaf individuals like they were surrounded with at school. One way adult deaf Americans began to socialize was by attending weekly worship services at hearing churches that provided interpreted services or by attending one of the few churches for the deaf."[68]

Since Deaf people live almost entirely in the world of the hearing, there is often a strong desire to be among other Deaf people. The complications and frustrations of living in a hearing-dominated and hearing-structured world necessitated support structures in the forms of clubs, newspapers, and networks. A shared discourse about a common experience of exclusion and oppression developed, and a sense of shared identity was established. At the heart of this identity was religion. Morse submits, "Religious training maintained importance at deaf residential schools well into the twentieth century. Chapel services transmitted not only the deaf community's value of sign language but perpetuated a deaf identity that exuded morality."[69]

In addition to the efforts of hearing people to evangelize deaf people, again related to the influence of the residential schools, were many deaf missions to the deaf and many deaf evangelists. For example, Phillip J. Hasenstab was a deaf minister who directed the Chicago Mission from the 1890s to 1941. Hasenstab traveled throughout the Midwest in evangelistic campaigns and "to some, he was the embodiment of God."[70] To give some idea of the impact of Hasenstab and his contemporaries, consider that some deaf circuit riders traveled twelve hundred miles and visited an average of more than thirty-three locations per month to preach to deaf people throughout the Midwest.[71]

Mission and evangelism in the nineteenth and most of the twentieth century followed the residential schools either in model or geography. Either the schools were themselves the vehicle of evangelism as Gallaudet had imagined, or they became the centers around which other evangelistic ministries, Deaf churches, or Deaf ministries were oriented. However, a series of educational acts intended to mainstream people with disabilities had the unfortunate consequence of breaking apart what had been brought together in the form of residential schools for the Deaf. The Rehabilitation Act of 1973,

---

[68]Morse, "Seeing Grace," 73-74.
[69]Ibid., 136.
[70]Olney, "Chicago Mission for the Deaf," 175.
[71]Ibid., 197.

Section 504, and the Education for All Handicapped Children Act of 1975 (PL 94-142), later named the Individuals with Disabilities Education Act (IDEA), were aimed to address, among other things, the problem of warehousing students with disabilities in institutions and separating them from their developing peers. What seemed like a new day to many disabled students and their families was perceived very differently by many in the Deaf community. The acts proposed that children be educated in the least restrictive environment. According to Van Cleve and Crouch,

> Perhaps the most serious of these was the Education for All Handicapped Children Act of 1975. This seemingly benign amendment to an earlier law authorizing federal support programs to benefit handicapped children, required that handicapped children be educated in the "least restrictive environment." This could be interpreted to mean that deaf children should not be placed in residential schools with other deaf students.[72]

Van Cleve and Crouch lament that the act, intended to help those perceived as disabled to relate to the "normal" world, had an adverse effect on the Deaf community in that it decimated "the institution most responsible for socializing deaf children into the adult deaf community."[73]

Deaf Diaspora

Until the 1970s, residential schools were the targets of ecclesial and parachurch Deaf ministries. The residential schools were surrounded by satellite Deaf ministries that relied on the students' exposure to sign language, drew on the religious component of education, and leveraged intergenerational relationships to develop ministries to the Deaf. However, the loss of a central hub, the residential school, meant both changes in Deaf culture and in Deaf ministry and mission. In Bob Ayres's opinion, the Deaf diaspora has brought about "a crisis of culture, language, relationships, and faith."[74] More specifically, he states, "The homeland is vanishing, the language is in a state of flux, and whatever shared values existed previously are being greatly altered by more frequent contact with the majority hearing

---

[72]Van Cleve and Crouch, *Place of Their Own*, 171.
[73]Ibid.
[74]Bob Ayres, *Deaf Diaspora: The Third Wave of Deaf Ministry* (New York: iUniverse, 2004), 4.

population."[75] Aside from the challenges in the United States, consider the challenges worldwide according to a 2015 DOOR International document, "Reaching the Largest Unreached People Group You Never Considered: White Paper on Reaching the Deaf Worldwide with the Gospel": out of 70 million Deaf people worldwide, only 2 percent of them are Christians, according to their metrics.[76]

While it is true, as Schreiter urges, that "localism and contextualization in themselves do not guarantee a greater truth,"[77] it is also true that culturally diverse expressions of the gospel enrich the church's conception and experience of the kingdom of God. The problem is that when we consider Deaf gain in terms of contextualization of the gospel, we must also remain aware of power dynamics and be attuned to the ways that difference has been homogenized, colonized, demonized, romanticized, and even pluralized into negation.

At the beginning of this chapter I attempted to complexify notions of d/Deaf culture by pointing out that even hearing people can participate (CODA or children of Deaf adults who enter the Deaf world through close connection to sign language). Unfortunately, d/Deaf persons and hard-of-hearing persons are often grouped together as "the deaf" and *homogenized* into a disabled group of defective persons, as I suggested above when I explained the cultural construction of "the deaf" as "disabled." When a group is homogenized, they can be more easily dismissed, and their contributions lost to the church.

Similarly, d/Deaf people have been *colonized*. Simply browsing writings by Deaf people, it is easy to discern that d/Deaf people feel colonized by an audist culture. For example, the uncritical and wide acceptance of the notion that sound is nearly exclusively an acoustic phenomenon is just one way that d/Deaf people have had to live in a world dominated, and one could say colonized, by a hearing hermeneutic. But hearing people need others to help them to learn that sound isn't merely an acoustic phenomenon—it is also "an organization of meaning around a variation in the physical world."[78]

---

[75]Ibid., 12.

[76]DOOR International, "Reaching the Largest Unreached People Group You Never Considered," October 2015, http://docplayer.net/29124003-Reaching-the-largest-unreached-people-group -you-never-considered-white-paper-on-reaching-the-deaf-worldwide-with-the-gospel.html.

[77]Schreiter, "Teaching Theology from an Intercultural Perspective," 15.

[78]Carol Padden and Tom Humphries, *Deaf in America: Voices from a Culture* (Cambridge, MA: Harvard University Press, 1988), 92.

Furthermore, our understanding of the meaning of sound is tied to cultural practices. Not to recognize this and to privilege a certain interpretation of sound as normative and prescriptive is audist.

Deaf people know that sound exists and can feel the reverberations of the frequencies. Deaf people know that there are sounds, but they don't necessarily know how those sounds will be interpreted unless they learn this from hearing people—for example, a cough versus a burp or passing gas. Why does one sound elicit one reaction and another a different reaction? It is because "the realm of sound very often involves issues of control."[79] Sound belongs to hearing people! However, Deaf people can discern harmony, variation, resonance, and dissonance. My childhood friend Paul, who was oral Deaf, bought Def Leppard's chart-topping *Pyromania* cassette tape in the mid-1980s and participated in the phenomenon of enjoying the ultra-produced song "Photograph" by resting his hand on his boom box as it blared. He had a legitimate encounter with the music that few if any of his hearing peers understood or appreciated.

Deaf people have always faced misunderstanding from hearing people who have at least marginalized them and at times *demonized* them or the condition of deafness. Aristotle, whose thinking would have a deep impact on Christian theology, wrote over three hundred years before Jesus walked the earth, "Those who are born deaf become senseless and incapable of reason."[80] Augustine, approximately four hundred years after Jesus' birth, made comments that were interpreted by the church in a way that is equally troubling for d/Deaf people. The translation reads, "But, since you also deny that any infant is subject to original sin, you must answer why such great innocence is sometimes born blind; sometimes deaf. Deafness is a hindrance to faith itself, as the Apostle says: 'Faith is from hearing.'"[81] There is debate about both the accuracy of the translation and about what Augustine meant, and there is a rich history of arguments that have debunked the notion that Augustine ever communicated that deaf

---

[79]Ibid., 100.

[80]Jack Gannon, Jane Butler, and Laura-Jean Gilbert, eds., *Deaf Heritage: A Narrative History of Deaf America* (Silver Spring, MD: National Association of the Deaf, 1981), xxv. Thanks to Tom Hudspeth for leading me to this resource.

[81]Saint Augustine, *Against Julian*, 115, quoted in Jon K. Ashby, "Alexander Campbell on Evangelizing the Deaf," *Restoration Quarterly* 24 (1981): 13.

people could not have faith.[82] There is, however, no question that an interpretation of Augustine that is unfavorable to d/Deaf people has been perpetuated and persisted.

In what was actually part of a larger argument about the pervasive impact of his notion of original sin, Augustine's interpretation of deafness primarily in terms of sin and defect demonized deafness for centuries to come: "'[Augustine] states that the presence of defects (blindness, deafness, etc.) in children are evidence of original sin. If original sin did not exist, why the punishment of innocent children. . . . ' How could the image of God be so adorned?"[83] At what point is a difference a defect? Who decides? My sense is that Deaf Christians don't necessarily have an issue with a doctrine that suggests humans are sinful and that sin impacts all aspects of our being, our relationships, and our environment. But they would challenge the idea that their deafness and Deaf culture is evidence of a fallen state any more than having blue eyes versus brown eyes would be.

Beyond the contribution of Aristotle and interpretation of Augustine, we have the words attributed to Jesus in the Markan account of the gospel, "When Jesus saw that a crowd came running together, he rebuked the unclean spirit, saying to it, 'You spirit that keeps this boy from speaking and hearing, I command you, come out of him, and never enter him again!'" (Mk 9:25). Based on such accounts in the Gospels, d/Deaf people are made to be the battlefields of a cosmic conflict, and deafness is directly connected to evil spirits. Biblical interpretations that make simple moves from the text to the context of contemporary d/Deaf people present significant challenges to including and appreciating the gifts of d/Deaf people in congregations.

Equally troubling is the fact that many hearing people who encounter sign language today tend to *romanticize* it as a special, sacred language. Noah Buchholz, a theologically trained Deaf ASL storyteller, poet, speaker, and Bible translator, explained it to me this way:

> Aesthetically speaking, through sign language God's Word is proclaimed visually. This can be beautiful and inspiring. Interestingly, many hearing people

---

[82]See Edward Allen Fay, "What Did St. Augustine Say?," in *American Annals of the Deaf* 58 (1912).
[83]Ashby, "Alexander Campbell on Evangelizing the Deaf," 13.

told me that they believe that sign language embodies God's Word while spoken language cannot. I'm not sure how I feel about this. Sign language and spoken language are both a language. Yes, there are some things you can get from sign language that you cannot get from spoken language. Yes, sign language is multidimensional while spoken language is linear. But, that doesn't enable sign language to embody God's Word. When they see God's Word being proclaimed in sign language, people might say, "Aha! We've found a way to embody God's Word!" Embodying God's Word goes beyond language. I'd not say sign language embodies God's Word; it simply proclaims God's Word more visually.[84]

Deafness has been understood by hearing people as a special capacity. As Fernandes explains of the nineteenth century, "Not only was sign language an instrument of evangelism, as a means of providing religious instruction to the deaf, but it could also serve all people as a way to reveal and communicate the presence of the eternal soul."[85] This belief corresponded to the belief that the deaf were somehow naturally closer to the experience of the original humans. Sign language was seen as an "original language of mankind"; it was a "language closer to God and nature than speech, uncorrupted and pure, more honest because more direct as a means of emotional expression."[86] Another issue from the perspective of some Deaf people, related to romanticizing Deaf culture and ASL, is that of cultural and language appropriation. Well-meaning parishioners might find visual language inspiring and disconnect it from the concrete context of the life and history of Deaf people.[87]

Finally, as with all differences, d/Deafness can be *pluralized* by hearing Christians wishing to connect with d/Deaf persons such that the genuine differences in the d/Deaf experience and Deaf culture are not acknowledged or appreciated. When this happens, the church unwittingly participates in further marginalizing a Deaf contribution to theology, ministry, and witness in the name of inclusion. The epigram "We are all disabled" may be used to gloss over real differences in perception, hermeneutics, and communication.

---

[84]Personal correspondence, March 23, 2016.
[85]Fernedes, *Gate to Heaven*, 195.
[86]Baynton, *Forbidden Signs*, 9.
[87]Thanks to Noah Buchholz for this insight.

DEAF GAIN AND MISSIOLOGY

In what follows I will address d/Deaf culture using the same missiological categories that I introduced in the previous chapter. I will use the missiological concepts *missio Dei*, indigenous appropriation and contextualization, and witness to examine potential Deaf gain, and will imagine the enrichment that comes to the church when it has a true encounter with diversity.

Missio Dei. As I explained above, *missio Dei* is a concept that developed in the 1950s to place the emphasis in mission theology back on the initiative of the triune God and take it away from troubled and contested expressions of missions. As the church discerns God's redemptive work in the world and joins it, the church receives an added benefit. As the church joins God's mission in the world and sees the Holy Spirit at work beyond expectations and beyond the resources and understanding of the church, our comprehension of the gospel is enlarged and enriched. People from various cultures backgrounds, in different social settings, and with diverse understandings of the world bring their converted treasures into the church. To apply this insight to the argument of this book, people with limited physical, emotional, mental, intellectual, and sensory abilities (i.e., everyone) add something to the church's understanding of the gospel when they are impacted by the mission of God and respond out of their own circumstances and setting.

When we consider d/Deaf people and Deaf culture from the perspective of *missio Dei*, we should expect to find Deaf gains to our understanding of the gospel rather than obstacles. Deaf gain has been defined as "the notion that the unique sensory orientation of Deaf people leads to a sophisticated form of visual-spatial language that provides opportunities for exploration into the human character."[88] With a Deaf perspective comes new understandings of human diversity and how humans respond to the initiative of God. It involves a redefinition of language to be a different kind of medium for communicating and developing community, appreciation for bilingual environments, opportunities to explore the visual, spatial, and kinetic dimension of language,[89] and

---

[88]H-Dirsken L. Bauman and Joseph J. Murray, "Deaf Studies in the 21st Century: 'Deaf-Gain' and the Future of Human Diversity," in *The Disability Studies Reader*, ed. Lennard J. Davis (New York: Routledge, 2013), 247.

[89]Ibid., 249.

perhaps even clarity in communication. Bauman and Murray assert that visual-spatial language "does not lack in abstraction, but gains in clarity of the concrete representation of complex ideas."[90]

One particularly important point for directly connecting mission studies and disability studies/Deaf studies is the fact that as the center of Christianity has been shifting southward, so seemingly is there a corresponding shift in the "central loci of Deaf studies."[91] As African, Asian, and Latino/a experiences begin to generate the questions that guide mission theology into the next decades, those questions are more likely to intersect with the human experience of deafness and Deaf cultures. As Bauman and Murray explain,

> An expanded frame of reference will naturally include the global South, which will have an increasingly prominent role in transnational Deaf communities of the future, especially if current demographic analyses regarding developed countries trend as predicted. Economic disparities between the North and South have resulted in lesser rates of cochlear implantation, less use of genetic testing, and hindrances in the prevention of childhood illnesses, all of which have the result of expanding the population of deaf children and potentially native signers.[92]

Missio Dei, the missionary activity of God, finds human correspondence in the process of contextualizing theology and through the witness of the church. I will explore these below.

Indigenous appropriation, contextualization, and witness. Translation of Scripture into vernacular languages has been one of the time-tested methods of Christian expansion for Protestants. As we have noted, Gallaudet was committed to sign language because he felt it was the most suitable form of communication to convey the truth of Scripture to deaf people. However, when I use the term *expansion* I have more in mind than Gallaudet's goal of increasing the number of adherents to the Christian faith. Certainly the process of translation has been an important tool in the expansion of the faith. And since Protestants were committed to producing translations of the Bible in the native tongue, education facilities accompanied these translated Scriptures in order that native populations might

---

[90]Ibid.
[91]Ibid., 253.
[92]Ibid., 252.

access its contents. However, beyond the understanding of translation that privileges the institutions and initiatives of the West, mission scholars such as Andrew Walls, Lamin Sanneh, Kwame Bediako, and David Barrett present translation as a missiological phenomenon that forces missionaries to work with native peoples and in fact privileges indigenous agency in creating and later appropriating vernacular Scriptures. In this way the translation of the Bible into non-Western languages (and sign language) results in new expressions of the faith—expressions that are necessary if Christianity is to expand into the fullness of its pluriform witness in the world. As a general overview we can examine the translation theories of Andrew Walls, Lamin Sanneh, and Kwame Bediako, and then look more closely at the underappreciated work of David Barrett. I will then make connections between the issues addressed in translating Scripture and the possibilities and missiological significance of translating and contextualizing the Christian message into Deaf categories.

Andrew Walls likens translation to the incarnation by means of John 1:14: "And the Word became flesh and lived among us, and we have seen his glory." The incarnation, he maintains, was God's chosen medium of self-communication. God was not translated into impersonal flesh—there is no such thing as general humanity. God was translated, in Jesus, into a specific segment of social reality: a Palestinian Jew with a Galilean accent marginalized from the center of the world's power stage. When Jesus' words—which, by the way, were neither spoken nor recorded in the "holy" language of the temple—were translated from Aramaic to Greek in the Scriptures, another act of translation, fully dependent on the first, took place.[93]

This process continues today as Scripture is translated into non-Western languages and sign languages. Furthermore, when a translation is made, it must take into account the worldview of the culture into which the Bible is being translated. Words and signs, pregnant with meaning, are chosen to convey concepts such as grace, mercy, and forgiveness in a Christian way, and in the process new meanings and accents accrue. Parts of Scripture that have been deemphasized in one historical context find new life in another. Walls relates this concept in his article "The Gospel as Prisoner and

---

[93]Andrew F. Walls, *The Missionary Movement in Christian History: Studies in the Transmission of Faith* (Maryknoll, NY: Orbis Books, 1995), especially chap. 3.

Liberator of Culture."[94] He offers the image of a theater in which everyone sees the same show from a different seat. The perspectives represent cultural biases that are a part of our limited perceptions. All of the perspectives are essential so that as a community, all of the theatergoers might have a more comprehensive understanding of the show. Scripture translated into non-Western languages allows those who speak that language a seat in the theater. The more that non-Western Christians are equipped with Scripture to make their own responses, the greater the opportunity for what Walls calls an "Ephesian moment." In the Ephesian moment, reconciliation is visibly demonstrated as people from different cultural backgrounds share in one communion. This process leads to the fullness or expansion of the Christian faith.

One concrete example of the creative dynamics Walls is recognizing—but from a Deaf culture perspective rather than one that is geographically cross-cultural—is a Deaf interpretation of Mark 7, what is likely known by hearing interpreters as the miraculous account of Jesus healing a deaf man. Fr. Thomas Coughlin, a Deaf Dominican, argues that the account of Jesus healing the deaf man in Mark 7 is less about the man receiving "healing" and more about the man receiving a commission. "When Jesus commanded a deaf man to 'open up,'" Coughlin explains, "Jesus was actually instituting a mission of ministry for deaf people."[95] Interestingly, and making the point that we can't homogenize Deaf people, I had two different Deaf readers offer two very different appraisals of Coughlin's interpretation. One communicated, "I've always liked this interpretation. . . . I always try to insert this perspective," and the other responded, "I personally don't feel comfortable with Coughlin's interpretation of Mark 7. I think it is disempowering for Deaf people on several levels."

The *ephphatha* command given by Jesus, Coughlin claims, is the first instance of a religious leader calling a deaf person to "be opened" to God's truth and to take responsibility as a herald of the gospel. He further makes

[94]Andrew F. Walls, "The Gospel and Prisoner and Liberator of Culture," in *Missionary Movement in Christian History*, 3-15.

[95]Thomas Coughlin, "Ephphatha: A Challenge or Deaf People's Responsibility for Deaf Ministry," in *The Gospel Preached by the Deaf: Proceedings from a Conference on Deaf Liberation Theology Held at the Faculty of Theology of the Catholic University of Leuven (Belgium), May 19th, 2003*, ed. Marcel Broesterhuizen (Leuven: Peeters, 2007), 15.

the connection to the providence of God in establishing Gallaudet University to "open up the horizons of deaf people." Their motto, taken from Mark's Gospel, is "Ephphatha: Be Thou Opened."[96] Jesus could have ministered to the deaf man by commanding his friends to look after his needs, but instead he addressed the deaf man and called him into ministry.[97] Certainly, Fr. Coughlin's experience of deafness and participation in Deaf culture—or his seat in the theater, as Walls has phrased it—has formed his hermeneutical framework and allowed him to see and hear something that is lost on hearing interpreters.

Another example of a Deaf cultural perspective potentially enriching the church comes from a conversation I recently had with Chad Entinger, a Deaf man who is the executive director of Deaf Mission. He was explaining that sign language can help hearing people to develop deeper understandings of Scripture and a different view of the world. He noted, as a culturally bilingual person (at home in both the Deaf and hearing worlds), that the Deaf community communicates in ways that are more visual and kinesthetic. They rely on body language and a self-understanding that is more collective or group oriented. In his experience, they tend to be more intimate and warm. He then mentioned the beginning of Acts as an example, and my mind went immediately to Pentecost and the affirmation of unity in diversity. Instead, he tried to help me imagine Acts 2:42-47, the first account of the post-Pentecost church. What was most interesting was that rather than telling me about the activities they shared—a hearing person might extract certain practices to be applied in the present context—he tried to help me to imagine their body language and disposition.

Where Walls emphasizes the incarnation to address issues of translation and indigenization, Sanneh draws on the Acts account of the event of Pentecost. For Sanneh, Pentecost represents the theological enfranchisement of the mother tongue.[98] In contrast to Islam, maintains Sanneh, Christianity does not have a sacred language. From the beginning Christianity has relativized yet retained certain aspects of its Jewish heritage and has destigmatized and promoted aspects of Gentile culture. This crossing of the Gentile

---

[96]Ibid., 16.
[97]Ibid., 23.
[98]Sanneh, *Translating the Message.*

frontier, along with the theological support of Pentecost, becomes paradigmatic for all future translations. Therefore, Sanneh gives attention to vernacular translations and the agency of the indigenous population in that
process. When a translator attempts to put the message in another's terms,
that translator must make certain concessions. To ask, "What is your word
for God?" is to tacitly admit that there may be more to God than what the
translator holds to be the case. In the process of the translation of the Bible
into non-Western languages, our perception of God's self-revelation is "ex-
panded." To ignore this fact is to make normative and prescriptive what is
otherwise a syncretistic achievement.

By focusing on vernacular translation and indigenous agency, Sanneh
was continuing and advancing the groundbreaking work that David Barrett
had begun two decades earlier. In *Schism and Renewal* (1968), mission
scholar David Barrett attempted to offer the first overall theory of African
independency. In summary, Barrett's conclusion can be expressed by the
following three points. First, as Stephen Neill points out in the introduction
to the work, translation of the Scriptures into the vernacular offered Africans a standard for evaluating the actions of missionaries that was independent of missionary control. As Neill notes,

> One of his [Barrett's] most interesting observations relates to the publication
> of the Scriptures in a local language and an independency movement. At the
> start, the missionary was the sole and absolute authority; he alone had access
> to the sources and his word was accepted as infallible. The moment the Af-
> rican Christian could read the Bible and especially the Old Testament for
> himself, he found himself introduced to a world much more closely resem-
> bling his own than the world of the European.[99]

In Barrett's own words,

> Up to this point the missions had had the same absolute control over the
> scriptures as they had exercised over the Church. They alone had access to
> the Hebrew and Greek sources; their interpretation was final. But with the
> publication of African translations, a momentous change took place: it now
> became possible to differentiate between missions and scriptures. Through

---

[99]David B. Barrett, *Schism and Renewal in Africa: An Analysis of Six Thousand Contemporary Religious Movements* (Nairobi: Oxford University Press, 1968), xv.

these scriptures God, Africans perceived, was addressing them in the vernacular in which was enshrined the soul of their people; but a large proportion of the missionary force still had not learned the vernacular, and addressed them in foreign tongues. The vernacular scriptures therefore provided an independent standard of reference that African Christians were quick to seize on.[100]

Second, based on this independent standard the Africans concluded that the missionaries were mounting an illegitimate attack on African society, in particular the family. They reacted by forming independent churches. Finally, Barrett concludes, the whole movement can be comprehended as a reaction to a failure of love by the missionaries: love expressed in terms of paternalism rather than *philadelphia*; the inability to differentiate the good from the bad in African culture (or their own); and the inability to make connections between the worldview of the Bible and the African worldview.

Another significant factor, one that has parallels in the missionary engagement with d/Deaf people, was that the missionaries' apologetic was not one of fulfillment, like many of the early church fathers; instead, theirs was a message of replacement and destruction of indigenous culture. (See William Jennings's critique in *The Christian Imagination*.)[101] Gallaudet manifested both a high view of the deaf person and sign language while at the same time evincing values of Western culture that stamped out difference in order to create a homogenous citizenry. Gallaudet was participating in a process of incarceration (limiting the freedom of deaf people in creating a genuine Deaf culture) through his unwavering commitment to audist/ableist American values. At the same time he provided the tools for the deaf to become Deaf, overcome those limitations, and create an identity in creative tension with the hearing community. For Barrett, a similar paradox is the key to understanding African independence:

> The attitude of destruction was accompanied by, for the first time in history, a massive endeavour to give that society full facilities for judging the legitimacy of the destructive assault—namely, the Christian scriptures translated into four hundred African languages. This remarkable paradox will

---

[100]Ibid., 127.

[101]Willie James Jennings, *The Christian Imagination: Theology and the Origins of Race* (New Haven, CT: Yale University Press, 2011).

now be shown to have led directly to a phenomenon also unique in the history of Christian missions—the rise of independency in Africa on a continental scale.[102]

Access to the Bible in their vernacular gave Africans the freedom to create an African Christian theology, a liberating theology that created an authentic African Christian identity. Sign language as a religion-bearing language did the same for the Deaf.

Ghanaian theologian Kwame Bediako contends that having the Scriptures in the vernacular increases the likelihood that Africans will respond to African problems in African terms and will discover African solutions. The fact that certain Old Testament figures had several wives, that Jesus communed with the long-deceased Moses and Elijah, and that the world of the New Testament is more akin to the African world than the European all serve to exonerate the African life-world from Western attacks. The translation of the Bible into non-Western languages, from Bediako's standpoint, allows the African to recover the past—and no one has an identity without a past.[103] Through the process of translation into the Deaf vernacular, Deaf people continue to have similar personal connections to the biblical narratives for the sake of developing a Deaf Christian identity.

When the Bible is translated into the communicative and linguistic modes of Deaf culture, it is translated into sign language or drama. Bob Ayres, the founder of what has become a Deaf youth ministry arm of Youth for Christ, relates a drama that summarizes that power of Scripture for liberation along the lines of Walls, Sanneh, and Barrett:

> The details are sketchy but it was a drama performed during a national convention of Deaf ministry with a major denomination. On the stage were Deaf people, in the role of marionettes attached by strings and under control of hearing puppeteers. The hearing people were controlling every movement of these Deaf Christians. Then, someone used a Bible to symbolically cut the strings and release the Deaf individuals to stand independently and assume control of their own lives and ministry.[104]

---

[102]Barrett, *Schism and Renewal*, 89.
[103]See Kwame Bediako, *Christianity in Africa: The Renewal of a Non-Western Religion* (Maryknoll, NY: Orbis, 1996), and Bediako, *Theology and Identity*.
[104]Ayres, *Deaf Diaspora*, 88.

What are some of the things we the church can learn from dialogue with d/Deaf people and culture that can impact the overall *witness* of the church? As this chapter has demonstrated, enhanced communication, embodiment, different and more relational ways of arranging space, visual-kinetic ways of communicating the gospel, and an emphasis on community are all Deaf gains to the witness of the church.

4

Intellectual Disabilities and
Our Iconic Witness

In his moving work *Adam: God's Beloved*, Henri Nouwen gives an account of his move from being a professor at Harvard to being a resident at Daybreak, a L'Arche community near Toronto where he shared life with people with profound intellectual and developmental disabilities. In particular, he shares of his relationship with Adam, "the weakest person of our family,"[1] a twenty-five-year-old man who could provide no self-care. He describes him this way: "Adam did not have unique heroic virtues: he did not excel in anything that newspapers write about. But I am convinced that Adam was chosen to witness to God's love through his brokenness."[2] While Nouwen is determined not to romanticize Adam in his account, at times he surely does. However, he also raises important questions about how people with intellectual and developmental disabilities participate in the Christian practice of bearing witness.

The purpose of this chapter is to offer another concrete example of how I imagine reorienting the conversation about disability and mission. I have already offered a general introduction to many of the important theological and missiological issues raised by the lived experience of disability, and we have uncovered some of the ableist biases inherent in missiology and the church's witness. In this chapter I will consider intellectual disabilities (ID) as a focal point for thinking through missiology and witness. In the process I will add theological depth to Nouwen's reflections on Adam's witness.

---

[1] Henri J. M. Nouwen, "Adam's Story: The Peace That Is Not of This World," in *Seeds of Hope: A Henri Nouwen Reader*, ed. Robert Durback (New York: Image, 1997), 255.
[2] Henri J. M. Nouwen, *Adam: God's Beloved* (Maryknoll, NY: Orbis, 1997), 30.

One of the unique complications with ID and theology is that persons with ID are sometimes theologized out of significance due their limited capacities for abstraction and rationality, which are deemed essential to being a person, participating in imaging God, or being a witness. Consequently, many theologians who address ID or profound disabilities wrestle with the concepts of the image of God and personhood.[3]

Finally, given that the image (or *eikōn*) of God is such a contested issue for people with ID, I will offer an appropriation of Orthodox theologies of evangelism and witness as understood from Orthodox missiologists and

---

[3]Molly Haslam, Thomas Reynolds, Hans Reinders, and Amos Yong, for example, are all leaders in this discussion who feel the need to address the image of God, theological anthropology, and personhood. I will engage them below. For a more recent publication, see Jill Harshaw, *God Beyond Words: Christian Theology and the Spiritual Experiences of People with Profound Intellectual Disabilities* (London: Jessica Kingsley, 2016).

theologians of iconography. I term this approach "iconic witness," and I promote it as a way of appreciating some of the ways that people with intellectual and developmental disabilities participate in bearing the witness of the Spirit in modes that aren't necessarily rational or linear, programmatic, or dependent on the capacity for abstraction or verbal communication.

Intellectual Disabilities

Including all that has been discussed above about disability generally, intellectual disability, according to the American Association on Intellectual and Developmental Disabilities (AAIDD), is qualified as "a disability characterized by significant limitations in both *intellectual functioning* and in *adaptive behavior*, which covers many everyday social and practical skills."[4] People with intellectual disabilities make up approximately 4 percent of the population. The challenges faced by people with intellectual disabilities include difficulties related to language and literacy, interpersonal skills, occupational skills, and personal care skills.

However, the greatest problem seems to be that people with intellectual disabilities, especially profound disabilities, seem so "other" that many people simply cannot imagine accepting them as they are. "Not many people in our society believe that spending time with an intellectually disabled person will contribute to the 'quality' of their lives," explains ethicist Hans Reinders.[5] Western culture's vision of the "good life" does not include sharing life with the intellectually disabled. Reinders states profoundly, "What ultimately prevents people with intellectual disabilities from full participation in our society is the fact that they are generally not seen as people we want to be present in our lives. We don't need them. . . . They are rarely chosen as friends."[6] Even the church, instead of imagining life together with people with intellectual disabilities and considering that our mutual encounter might result in changes in discipleship, ministry, and witness, Christians tend to follow the marginalizing approaches that Schrieter describes as homogenizing, colonizing, demonizing, romanticizing, or pluralizing.

---

[4] "Definition of Intellectual Disability," American Association on Intellectual and Developmental Disabilities, accessed March 11, 2018, aaidd.org/intellectual-disability/definition#.VyJiaKudvww.
[5] Hans S. Reinders, *Receiving the Gift of Friendship: Profound Disability, Theological Anthropology, and Ethics* (Grand Rapids: Eerdmans, 2008), 7.
[6] Ibid., 142.

The church follows the dominant culture in *homogenizing* people with ID. As should be clear by now, disability is a complex and heterogeneous concept, and ID is no different. It can be mild to profound; some people with intellectual disabilities can hold a job, and others can't hold a cup of tea. Some have the capacity to interact with others as self-determining agents, and others are responsive in ways that are barely discernible to those who don't spend hours with them. Within the church, people with ID should be empowered to participate in the life of the congregation to the extent that they desire and their capacities and gifts allow them, just like everyone else.

Exposés and documentaries have shown how people with ID have been *colonized*; they are often placed into residential facilities. Consider Geraldo Rivera's exposé of Willowbrook State School—less a school than a facility for warehousing children with intellectual disabilities.[7] In what can only be considered incarceration, fifty-three hundred patients/students were organized on the campus with a ratio of one attendant per seventy clients. One hundred percent of the residents contracted hepatitis, abuse and trauma were part of the daily curriculum, and there was almost no intellectual stimulation or life-skills training. While deinstitutionalization seeks to ensure nothing like Willowbrook will happen again on such a large scale, Liat Ben-Moshe expands the concept of incarceration to include "hospitalization, institutionalization and imprisonment and a fuller understanding of the forces that construct medicalization and criminalization."[8]

People with ID are occasionally *demonized*, and some are treated as threats. They are criminalized, especially if they have developmental disabilities or mental health concerns. A recent study in *Journal of Autism and Developmental Disorders* came to the following conclusion: "An interesting but controversial aspect of Asperger syndrome is its association with violent crime. Although Asperger used the label 'autistic psychopathy' as a stable personality style and not as an index of criminality, reports have continued to describe links between AS and violent crime."[9] Newman and Ghaziuddin's concerns were confirmed in the wake of Adam Lanza's mass shooting at Sandy Hook

---

[7]See Rivera's report at geraldo.com/page/willowbrook.
[8]Liat Ben-Moshe, "'The Institution Yet to Come': Analyzing Incarceration Through a Disability Lens," in *The Disability Studies Reader*, ed. Lennard J. Davis, 4th ed. (New York: Routledge, 2013), 133.
[9]Stewart S. Newman and Mohammad Ghaziuddin, "Violent Crime in Asperger Syndrome: The Role of Psychiatric Comorbidity," *Journal of Autism and Developmental Disorders* 38 (2008): 1848.

Elementary School when his Asperger's diagnosis was made public. Many news sources and blogs conflated Lanza's murderous motives with markers of autism, suggesting that his autism made him more criminally oriented since he possessed no capacity to feel remorse for or connect with others.[10] Recent first-person accounts by people on the autism spectrum have challenged such mischaracterizations,[11] but the mischaracterizations still leave powerful impressions on public perception.

People with ID are often *romanticized* as cute poster children, or through heartwarming stories of angelic "holy innocents" who are always joyful despite their circumstances. They are romanticized in the viral videos of adolescents with ID who "overcome" their disabilities and accomplish athletic feats, for example, in the playful critique of such videos in *Saturday Night Live*'s disturbing skit "Champ."[12] Some of these accounts raise awareness of the gifts and capabilities of people with ID, but others are framed in such a way that the disability community has harshly critiqued them as "inspiration porn."[13]

Finally, people with ID are *pluralized* when their real differences are glossed over by the idea that "we are all disabled." Of course, we are all on the dis/ability spectrum and share in being limited. But again, we cannot ignore the fact that people with ID experience real differences in how society treats them because of their impairments. When I asked my friend Seth, "What is one thing that you would want me to teach my students about people with Downs?" he answered unhesitatingly, "Respect! I want to be treated with respect." He has experienced people disrespecting him simply because he has Down syndrome. There are consequential differences in how

[10]David Wagner, "Adam Lanza, Asperger's, and the Media Narrative on Autism and the Mentally Ill," *Atlantic*, December 17, 2012, www.thewire.com/national/2012/12/adam-lanza-aspergers-autism-and-violence/60078/.

[11]For example, see John Elder Robison, *Look Me in the Eye: My Life with Asperger's* (New York: Three Rivers, 2007), and Naoki Higashida, *The Reason I Jump: The Inner Voice of a Thirteen-Year-Old Boy with Autism* (New York: Random House, 2013).

[12]Originally aired March 5, 2016.

[13]Comedian and journalist Stella Young coined the term "inspiration porn." She explained that to many in society, "[disabled people] are not real people, we are there to inspire." Simply living with a disability makes one exceptional in the eyes of others. She considers images that traffic in disability as inspiration porn when they objectify one group of people for the benefit of another—these images use representations of disability to communicate that "no matter how bad my life is, it could be worse. I could be that person." Stella Young, "Stella Young: I'm Not Your Inspiration, Thank You Very Much," www.youtube.com/watch?v=8K9Gg164Bsw.

people with ID experience the world because of their impairments. For example, unlike many other facets of the disability rights movements where independence is a goal, the self-advocacy movement for people with intellectual disabilities (People First) is dependent on people without intellectual disabilities. Intellectual disability, as Joseph Shapiro describes, "means that a person has much greater difficulty learning than others. So people with [intellectual disabilities] often need help in making the choices and judgment that constitute their own acts of self-assertion. Almost always, a self-advocacy chapter relies on a facilitator [an advisor without intellectual disabilities] who helps break down complicated information but who ideally leaves decision making to the advocates."[14]

All this being said, it could be the case that in Christian theology and seminaries, people with ID aren't being homogenized, colonized, demonized, romanticized, or pluralized but rather simply not represented or considered at all.

Concretely, in my preparation for this chapter, I did not find the issue of ID or disability in general addressed at any depth (and rarely at all!) in any of the works about the image of God or theological anthropology that I surveyed. One recent publication (approximately four hundred pages in an otherwise excellent manuscript) concludes with the apologetic tone, "We have hardly touched on culture as a typical human way of self-expression, we left unmentioned the mentally and physically challenged though they are part of the human family too. . . . That these points and others were hardly mentioned does not mean that they are unimportant but that space did not permit a more extensive treatment."[15] However, the thick volume did cover widowhood, stem cells, homosexuality, "lifestyle drugs," polygamy, reincarnation, environmental concerns, and more. What does this communicate to people with disabilities? The message is: "Though you are part of a group that makes up nearly 20 percent of the population, there still isn't room for you." How does the "null curriculum" of people with ID impact the reader's assumptions, expectations, and imagination?

---

[14]Joseph P. Shapiro, *No Pity: People with Disabilities Forging a New Civil Rights Movement* (New York: Three Rivers, 1994), 187.

[15]Hans Schwarz, *The Human Being: A Theological Anthropology* (Grand Rapids: Eerdmans, 2013), 383.

Since such a large percentage of the US population can be considered disabled, should not disability be foregrounded in our anthropologies as one of the ways humans are embodied, or at least engaged in recognition of human diversity instead of buried in an appendix or in a statement in the conclusion that explains its absence? In the texts I consulted, the overarching ableist bias is never questioned, and this fact has obvious consequences for the 4 percent of the population with ID, who are never represented.

THEOLOGICAL ANTHROPOLOGY WITH A MISSIOLOGICAL TWIST

Briefly stated, according to J. Patout Burns, "Theological anthropology investigates the resources, the limitations, and the destiny of the human person."[16] In the section that follows I will use Burns's categories as a guide to think through theological anthropology and intellectual disability. This has already been done well elsewhere by capable scholars (Thomas Reynolds, Molly Haslam, Amos Yong, and Jill Harshaw, among others). What is unique about this chapter is the emphasis on a missional anthropology: I will foreground a concern for vocation, our common participation in bearing the witness of the Spirit. As Michael Welker has helpfully stated, "More important, the awareness has to be cultivated again that God sustains creation for a great purpose, that human life is not just meant for a 'bad infinity' (Hegel) of as many days as physically possible on this earth, that God elects the human beings as caretakers of creation and as witnesses to God's glory."[17]

Therefore, while inquiring about the resources, limitations, and destiny of the human with intellectual disabilities, I will pay special attention to the purpose of the human as expressed through election: to be "witnesses to God's glory." At the same time I will be attending to ethicist Hans Reinders's directive to speak about people with profound intellectual disabilities without setting up a paradigm that demotes them to an anthropological "minor league."[18]

---

[16]J. Patout Burns, ed., *Theological Anthropology* (Philadelphia: Fortress, 1981), 1.

[17]Michael Welker, "Theological Anthropology Versus Theological Reductionism," in *God and Human Dignity*, ed. R. Kendall Soulen and Linda Woodhead (Grand Rapids: Eerdmans, 2006), 326.

[18]Hans S. Reinders, "Human Dignity in the Absence of Agency," in Soulen and Woodhead, *God and Human Dignity*, 122-23.

RESOURCES: THE HUMAN AS CREATURE

The Enlightenment, Cartesian individualism, and the modern scientific worldview have had a great impact on theological anthropologies in the West. The rational mind has regularly been understood to provide both the capacities and resources necessary for the human to be viewed as the bearer of the image of God as well as providing the primary distinction between humans and the rest of the created world. This is certainly not a new insight, but it has implications for how we understand the personhood of those with intellectual disabilities. The primacy of reason as human nature's animating capacity; the belief that humans and society can progress to perfection as expressed in development, technology, and modernization; and the belief that one's reason is that of an emancipated, autonomous individual have positively contributed to challenging uncritically accepted traditions. Optimistically, these ideas have provided the philosophical framework for living together amid different religions, beliefs, and ways of life. The shadow side of the Enlightenment, however, is that nonrational aspects of human nature tend to be undervalued.

Anthropology is often reduced in modernity to self-conscious subjectivity. The antidote to the exclusiveness and limited nature of this position is not to create another, equally reductionistic approach but rather to come up with a theological framework that can accommodate many different approaches to anthropology and that acknowledges the complexity of human existence.[19]

When certain dominant themes associated with the Enlightenment inform our anthropology, our notions of humanity, personhood, and image of God are found in individual resources, such as one's capacity for self-determination, purposive agency, and reason. Consequently, the shadow side of the Enlightenment ensures that people who don't fit in are considered to be a lesser humanity—even in theological anthropology. For example, the well-respected and prolific theologian Helmut Thielicke describes in his *Wer darf sterben?* a severely impaired person as an "off-duty image of God," suggesting that the person is somehow a lesser version of God's image.[20] Perhaps Christian theologians can agree that theological anthropologies should begin with the notion of humans as creatures created in the image of God—but here the debate begins, particularly with respect to persons with intellectual disabilities. For with Thielicke's assertion still echoing in our ears, consider theologian Thomas Reynolds's pointed question, "Do persons with disabilities signify a lack of wholeness, a deficiency that blights the image of God?"[21]

Historically, biblical and theological approaches to understanding the image of God have not offered much guidance in answering Reynolds's question. The biblical record notes that humanity is created in God's image but does not fill out the content regarding what that means. Generally, theologians have offered substantialist or relational approaches to the *imago Dei*.[22] A substantialist approach refers to the human being's inherent possession of certain qualities or capacities that make the human similar to God. However, cultures tend to valorize qualities that are esteemed in society and, in the case of the West, favor intellectual capacity or reason, moral agency,

---

[19]Welker, "Theological Anthropology," 317.

[20]Jürgen Moltmann, *God in Creation* (Minneapolis: Fortress, 1993), 350n32.

[21]Thomas E. Reynolds, *Vulnerable Communion: A Theology of Disability and Hospitality* (Grand Rapids: Brazos, 2008), 186.

[22]Paul Sands, "The Imago Dei as Vocation," *Evangelical Quarterly* 82, no. 1 (2010): 28-41.

or self-transcendence as that which separates us from creatures. This in turn tends to shape which qualities or capacities theologians emphasize as they explore the *imago Dei*. A stress on reason elevates one characteristic of human existence above others with equal claim to consideration as part of our being. Colin Gunton writes, "In particular, it encourages the belief that we are more minds than we are bodies, with all the consequences that that has: for example, in creating a non-relational ontology, so that we are cut off from each other and from the world by a tendency to see ourselves as imprisoned in matter."[23] Such an understanding of the image of God supports the conclusion that people with intellectual deficits are somehow flawed or less than full image bearers.

In the relational approach, the image of God does not indicate an inherent capacity or trait possessed by the creature. Instead the image of God is something that occurs dynamically as the result of the relationship between creature and creator; the creature does something: it images God. For Luther, imaging is an ongoing, dynamic relationship of faith and trust in God. For Calvin, it is being a mirror that properly reflects God because it is properly oriented toward God in obedience. "Only while the mirror actually reflects an object," explains D. J. Hall, "does it have the image of that object. There is no such thing in Calvin's thought as an imago dissociated from the act of reflecting."[24] This approach to understanding the image of God seems to hold more hope for including people with disabilities, although there is still the possibility of arguing that people with ID lack the capacities required to properly reflect the image of God. I will build on the relational approach while following the lead of Kathryn Tanner and others that Christ is the key to understanding the image of God in a way that is inclusive of all people. When it comes to Christian theological anthropology, what we have in common is not a certain capacity, whether an intrinsic ability or the aptitude to reflect; what we have in common is that we have no capacity to image God on our own apart from Christ.

---

[23]Colin Gunton, "Trinity, Ontology and Anthropology: Towards a Renewal of the Doctrine of the *Imago Dei*," in *Persons, Divine and Human: King's College Essays in Theological Anthropology*, ed. Christoph Schwöbel and Colin E. Gunton (Edinburgh: T&T Clark, 1991), 48.

[24]John Douglas Hall, *Imaging God: Dominion as Stewardship* (Grand Rapids: Eerdmans, 1986), 34.

I contend that our status as persons is more about our relationship to the One who makes us persons and the fact that God is acting toward us in a particular way than it is about discerning what a person is with reference to some thing or capacity that makes us persons.[25] In this view, in agreement with Tanner, Moltmann, and Reinders, being a human is a gift from God, and all of our resources depend on God's resolve such that, in Moltmann's phrasing, "by virtue of the relationship in which God puts himself . . . to men and women, the handicapped . . . person is also God's image in the fullest sense of the word, the image is in no way a diminished one."[26] Our identity as image bearers of God and as persons is founded on the gift and initiative of God and expressed in our ultimate connection to God and other persons (through Christ) such that no one is excluded.

Moltmann is giving theological expression to a widely acknowledged philosophical conclusion that personhood "has more to do with relationality than with substantiality and that the term stands closer to the idea of communion or community than to the conception of the individual in isolation or abstracted from communal embeddedness."[27] Theologian Stanley Grenz proposes that we must move from viewing people as centered selves (Enlightenment individualism) to understanding them in terms of *social personalism*. This shift is important for those with disabilities, who find themselves left out of many theological anthropologies, because this line of reasoning suggests that we are all important when it comes to being a person—all of our gifts, difficulties, abilities, personalities, interests, and passions. Bonhoeffer scholar Clifford Green frames Bonhoeffer's contribution to understanding personhood similarly and in contrast to the Cartesian notion of the person: "His paradigm is not 'cogito, ergo sum,' but 'I relate ethically to others, ergo sum.'"[28] Humans don't exist "immediately" through themselves but as they encounter others and take responsibility for them. In our concrete and lived relations with others we bear responsibility

---

[25]Ian A. McFarland, *Difference and Identity: A Theological Anthropology* (Cleveland, OH: Pilgrim, 2001), 9.

[26]Moltmann, *God in Creation*, 233.

[27]Stanley J. Grenz, *The Social God and the Relational Self: A Trinitarian Theology of the Imago Dei* (London: Westminster John Knox, 2001), 4. See also F. LeRon Shultz, *Reforming Theological Anthropology: After the Philosophical Turn to Relationality* (Grand Rapids: Eerdmans, 2003).

[28]Clifford J. Green, *Bonhoeffer: A Theology of Sociality*, rev. ed. (Grand Rapids: Eerdmans, 1999), 30.

for others (*Stellvertretung*) while not violating the barrier of their personhood such that Bonhoeffer can state, "Thus the individual exists only in relation to an 'other'; individual does not mean solitary. On the contrary, for the individual to exist, 'others' must necessarily be there."[29] In this account of personhood, persons are united with the social reality of Christ in the church, and the absence of persons with intellectual disabilities in our lives and congregations would then make us less complete as the body of Christ and leave us with a less credible witness.

While this book is focused on disability in the United States, this notion of personhood as social is common outside the West. In Archbishop Desmond Tutu's words, "We say a person is a person through other persons. We don't come fully formed into the world. We learn how to think, how to walk, how to speak, how to behave, indeed how to be human from other human beings. We need other human beings in order to be human. We are made for togetherness, we are made for family, for fellowship, to exist in a tender network of interdependence."[30] African philosopher John Mbiti agrees: "Whatever happens to the individual happens to the whole group, and whatever happens to the whole group happens to the individual. The individual can only say, 'I am because we are, since we are therefore I am.'"[31]

Returning to Western sources, John MacMurray's Gifford lectures cast light on this discussion. He attempts to reorient the conversation about personhood from egocentricity and theoretical abstraction, which is isolating and static, to action and agency, which is dynamic and participatory. "The idea of an isolated agent is self-contradictory," he explains. "Any agent is necessarily in relation to the Other. Apart from this essential relation he does not exist. But, further, the Other in this constitutive relation must be personal. Persons, therefore, are constituted by their mutual relation to one another."[32] As John Aves interprets MacMurray, "Personality against many modern conceptions is not achieved in isolation from or at the expense of others or by the development of certain faculties such as reason, or by the

---

[29]Dietrich Bonhoeffer, *Sanctorum Communio: A Theological Study of the Sociology of the Church*, Dietrich Bonhoeffer Works 1 (Minneapolis: Fortress, 2009), 51. Person is a relational concept; personhood is a socio-ethical, historical personhood.

[30]Desmond Tutu, *Hope and Suffering* (Grand Rapids: Eerdmans, 1984), 65.

[31]John Mbiti, *African Religion and Philosophy* (Oxford: Heinemann, 1990), 106.

[32]John MacMurray, *Persons in Relation* (New York: Harper and Brothers, 1961), 24.

conscious social acceptance of others. We simply cannot exist or be our-selves apart from others. We are simply created to be directed outwards in intentional activity to mutuality or friendship or communion."[33] Elsewhere, MacMurray explains that the mother plays an important role in constituting the personhood of the infant, who clearly does not possess the requisite resources for personhood of rational capacity or agency. Nonetheless, the infant can and does respond in some way to the mother. John Swinton makes a similar point about a person with dementia, who is no longer able to remember her history and identity yet is buoyed by her community of faith, which gathers around her and reminds her who and whose she is.[34]

In my experience, even those persons with profound intellectual and de-velopmental disabilities who appear to have no capacity for purposive agency or self-determination can participate in congregational life and bear witness to the kingdom of God if we only allow them a place to appear.[35] Along this line, Molly Haslam further reasons that our personhood or humanity (the way we image God) is to be discerned in relationships of mutual responsiveness, and she alerts us to how ableism disorients our ability to recognize and ap-preciate nonsymbolic and intuitive ways of responding.[36] Haslam concludes that the *imago Dei* in human beings is a relational concept that involves par-ticipating in a meeting between responsive partners. This can include verbal, intellectual interaction, symbolization, and complex intentionality.

But, Haslam argues, our personhood, or the way we participate in the image of God, is not located in these capacities. Nonsymbolic responsiveness and intuitive ways of knowing and being known are equally legitimate ways of participating in mutual relationships. So when we broaden the category of response to attend to the nonverbal, nonlinguistic, nonsymbolic ways in which people with intellectual disabilities and profound disabilities respond in faith, our understanding of God and each other will be enriched. Haslam's solution to the apparent problem of personhood and the *imago Dei*

---

[33]John Aves, "Persons in Relation: John MacMurray," in Schwöbel and Gunton, *Persons, Divine and Human*, 136.

[34]John Swinton, "Theology and Dementia," presentation at Summer Institute on Theology and Disability, www.youtube.com/watch?v=LrcWCs5WdoQ.

[35]Benjamin T. Conner, *Amplifying Our Witness: Giving Voice to Adolescents with Developmental Disabilities* (Grand Rapids: Eerdmans, 2012), 69.

[36]Molly C. Haslam, *A Constructive Theology of Intellectual Disability: Human Being as Mutuality and Response* (New York: Fordham University Press, 2012), 9.

in people with ID is to avoid either conceptualizing the image of God in a way that looks inside the individual (grounding the concept of the human in a particular capacity) or establishing the image-of-God concept outside the individual (grounding the concept of the human in the movement of the other toward us). Instead, she explains, "I suggest that we locate our understanding of human being not on one or the other side of the subject/object dichotomy but in the realm of 'the between.' We find our humanity in relationships of mutual responsiveness, in which individuals with profound intellectual disabilities participate as responders, albeit in nonsymbolic, nonagential ways."[37] Using the example of a fictional individual (Chan) as representative of people with profound intellectual disabilities, Haslam explains, "Although Chan may not be able to offer grace in the form of consciously choosing to enter into relationship he would be able to offer grace in the form of his bodied presence which I encounter and which calls for my response."[38] What Haslam is describing, a presence that elicits or evokes a response, is foundational to what I consider to be the evocative witness of people with ID.

An evocative witness can also be discerned in Christopher deVinck's *Power of the Powerless*. He depicts his brother as "on his back in bed for thirty-two years, in the same corner of his room, under the same window, beside the same yellow walls. He was blind, mute. His legs were twisted. He didn't have the strength to lift his head or the intelligence to learn anything."[39] Yet deVinck notes that while profoundly disabled people like his brother might not have determinative agency, they do possess the evocative power to influence and move other people. Drawing on Haslam and deVinck, it could be maintained that limitations in verbal and processing skills of persons with intellectual disabilities uncover other avenues for communication beyond linguistic modalities. It has the potential to open people up to knowledge that is communicated through emotion, intuition, and feeling. Favoring rational discourse, we choose not to develop or attend to such

---

[37]Ibid. Haslam also finds the concept of the image of God as mirror helpful, but only if "we understand what mirrors God to include not only responsiveness to God in the form of understanding God's commands and self-conscious obedience to them *but also responsiveness to the world around us in less cognitive, nonsymbolic ways*" (104, italics added).

[38]Ibid., 82.

[39]Christopher deVinck, *Power of the Powerless: A Brother's Legacy of Love* (Grand Rapids: Zondervan, 1995), 27-28.

capacities in order to communicate holistically because such communication (and the person who employs it) is not valued in our society. John Swinton admits that when it comes to discerning the activity of God, he is limited. He explains, "My hopeless dependence on my intellect for making sense of the world actually prevents me from even beginning to understand how God might be present with [my intellectually disabled friend] in any meaningful sense."[40] Anna Shurley draws on her extensive experience as a chaplain for children and adults with intellectual and developmental disabilities in conversation with the theology of Karl Barth to affirm, "While the shape of vocation differs from one person to another, the crucial function of vocation is common to all: God has called all people to be witnesses, through their particular vocations, to God's work in Jesus Christ.... The task of all people— including people with intellectual disabilities—is simply to proclaim the gospel with their whole being."[41] My point is that those persons with ID, even people with profound developmental disabilities who appear to have no capacity for purposive agency, self-determination, or abstraction, can participate in the congregation's calling to bear witness in evocative ways, as Haslam, deVinck, Shurley, and my own experience have made clear.

In fact, what many people view as limits might not really be limits at all, according to Amos Yong. Yong offers a Pentecostal perspective on this issue, suggesting, "The many tongues of Pentecost are indicative also of the many different ways in which God both reveals himself and interacts with the various sensory capacities of embodied human beings. This 'many tongues, many senses' hermeneutic also illuminates how God condescends to meet human beings with diverse levels of ability and disability."[42] In terms of theological anthropology, Yong reminds us that not having certain resources, or certain social or processing skills, does not disqualify one from bearing the activity and gifts and witness of the Spirit.

Despite the hopeful picture presented above, humanity, in our current condition, does not correspond to God's original intention or ultimate purpose for us as creatures. The limitation of our resources has little to do

---

[40]John Swinton, "Building a Church for Strangers," *Journal of Religion, Disability, and Health* 4, no. 4 (2001): 28.

[41]Anna Katherine Shurley, *Pastoral Care and Intellectual Disability: A Person Centered Approach* (Waco, TX: Baylor University Press, 2017), 16.

[42]Amos Yong, *The Bible, Disability, and the Church: A New Vision of the People of God* (Grand Rapids: Eerdmans, 2011) 15.

with our capacities and everything to do with the direction of our affections and our condition as sinful.

LIMITATIONS: HUMANS AS FALLEN

We cannot find the image of God by simply looking at creation—the key to understanding humanity is Jesus Christ, the one image of the invisible God (Col 1:15; 2 Cor 4:4; Heb 1:3). We must confess that all of humanity and every aspect of creation is impacted by sin and recognize that there is simply no exemption from sin in the form of "holy innocents" for persons with intellectual disabilities—people with intellectual disabilities need the intervention and grace of God like everyone else. The limitation of our resources in properly imaging God has to do with the direction and purity of our love and nothing to do with the fact that we have limits (physical, intellectual, sensory) as contingent creatures.

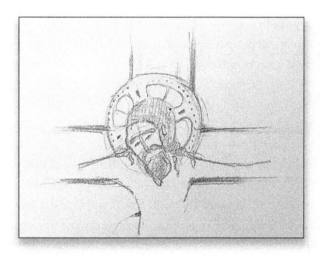

Deborah Creamer, who lives with a disabling condition, insists that limits are an unsurprising characteristic of human life; they are an intrinsic aspect of human existence that should be viewed as good, or at least should not be viewed in terms of evil, sin, or the fall. Creamer wants to reframe the question of disability in terms of diversity as opposed to deficiency. She explains that if we fail to understand our own limits, we tend to frame others' limits in terms of deficiencies related to sin. We also imagine heaven as the place where these deficiencies are overcome, and we subsequently invalidate the existence of persons with disabilities.[43]

Living in finitude, vulnerability, and contingency as a creature is limiting, but it is not sin. Further, it is impossible, given Jesus' words on the matter, to make a case that disability is the direct divine consequence of sin (one's own or one's family's sin): "His disciples asked him, 'Rabbi, who sinned, this man or his parents, that he was born blind?' Jesus answered, 'Neither this man nor his parents sinned'" (Jn 9:2-3). I am doubtful that we can characterize all of what our culture terms disability as a general result of the fall. Therefore, I strongly disagree with a conference speaker who stated, "Autism is like toxins and weeds: a result of the fall." To make matters worse, this individual was speaking to a room filled with people with disabilities, many of whom had friends on the autism spectrum. After hearing the distanced and clinical manner with which she spoke about people with autism when presenting her research, somebody asked her, "Do you have any friends with autism?" It wasn't a surprise when she answered that she did not.

A more balanced perspective is offered by Amy Julia Becker, who explains that there are aspects of her daughter's Down syndrome that seem to be products of sin or fallenness, mostly related to brokenness in relationships, but there are others that are "beautiful, life-giving and joyful." Down syndrome can't be "a particular demonstration of that fallenness and the brokenness that exists within our bodies."[44]

There are some characteristics of people with disabilities that, if they were absent, would seem to alter the personhood of the person. For example, my friend Dan relates to himself, others, the world, and God in a particular way because he has Down syndrome. Any community of faith would benefit from Dan's perspectives and gifts. Would Dan be Dan if he didn't have Downs? If John Elder Robison did not have Asperger's syndrome, then he might have been a more accomplished student, but KISS would not have had flaming guitars![45] On the other hand, my colleague Todd Billings, who has recently been struggling with cancer, has a different perspective. In order

---

[43]Deborah Beth Creamer, *Disability and Christian Theology: Embodied Limits and Constructive Possibilities* (Oxford: Oxford University Press, 2009), 94-95.

[44]Amy Julia Becker, "It's No Mistake, Penny Is Perfect," *Faith and Leadership*, February 6, 2012, www.faithandleadership.com/amy-julia-becker-its-no-mistake-penny-perfect.

[45]Robison, *Look Me in the Eye*.

to fight a disabling condition, cancer, he has chosen to voluntarily disable himself through chemotherapy. He had always experienced the world as a bright, energetic, and quick-witted person.[46] Now, though he will be quick to point out that his IQ has not changed (perhaps an attempt to hold on to who he knows himself to be while he experiences unsettling changes), he admits that he has difficulty benefiting from the value of it as his memory is compromised and he often experiences mental confusion related to chronic fatigue and neuropathy. What of these impairments is integral to his previously established identity? He would certainly be glad to be without them, and they seem to be related to the fallenness of this world. Nonetheless, they are a reminder to him that all of our incompleteness and brokenness are brought into God through Christ.

While there may be some debate on the relationship between human limitation and disability, it is excruciatingly obvious that structures of discrimination and exclusion (ablesim) are leveraged against people with intellectual and developmental disabilities. Such structures can certainly be understood in terms of the limiting consequences of human sin and fallenness. In fact, it would be simple to maintain that my friend Dan is limited less by his Down syndrome and its attendant complications than he is by structures of exclusion and ableism that subdue his flourishing. Or, again with reference to Dan, the physical, intellectual consequences of his Down syndrome are less of a disabling or limiting factor in his life and flourishing than his inability to offer forgiveness to someone if they hurt him. Like all other Christians, Dan will need to find his full humanity in Christ, limitations and all, in order to live into his destiny as part of God's creation.

Destiny: Humans in Christ, Bound to One Another, and Bearing Witness

The full realization of our humanity will occur when we see God. Phrased another way, "Humans are the image of God, properly speaking, only when actually contemplating God face to face in heaven."[47] Considering our destiny as humans in Christ is not simply a matter for the eschaton, though,

---

[46]See his extended engagement in J. Todd Billings, *Rejoicing in Lament: Wrestling with Incurable Cancer and Life in Christ* (Grand Rapids: Brazos, 2015).

[47]Kathryn Tanner, *Christ the Key* (Cambridge: Cambridge University Press, 2010), 4.

because all of us live into our humanity as we are united together (in all of our diversity) in Christ, the true image. According to Colin Gunton, the image of God that we bear together as we are united to each other and to Christ is not a static but dynamic possession that is "realised in the various relationships in which human life is set."[48]

Kathryn Tanner's important work on theological anthropology, *Christ the Key*, advances the notion that Jesus Christ is the true revelation of and the key to understanding human personhood. To understand what the image of God is and what a person is, Tanner argues that the proper image of God is the second person of the Godhead. We image God by attachment to or participation in the life of Jesus in the power of the Holy Spirit. As Christians

---

[48]Gunton, "Trinity, Ontology and Anthropology," 60-61.

we have an anemic anthropology if we do our thinking outside the revelation of image of God in Christ. Perhaps this is also the key for our theological anthropology. What we have in common is not a certain capacity but *no* capacity: "Human beings through divine power become what they are not and have no capacity of being by themselves: human versions of the divine image itself."[49]

Put another way, McFarland explains that we stand in a relationship that does not naturally exist. We cannot secure it for ourselves, and it is dependent on the prior act of God in Christ. And since everyone is brought in to this relationship through a unique relationship to Christ, difference is essential to personhood.[50] Thus we can simply echo Scripture—"Now you [plural] are the body of Christ and individually members of it" (1 Cor 12:27)—and confess our personhood is found collectively and *most abundantly* in our union with Christ and our connection to one another. The community of faith is enriched by the presence of people who respond in nonrational and intuitive ways, both through their contributions and perspectives and through the ways they evoke responses from others and help them live together into full personhood.

People with disabilities have more to add to the conversation about our destiny as humans in Christ than what they evoke in others. The late Nancy Eiesland, who lived with a disability and wrote extensively on the subject of disability and theology, suggested, "Our bodies participate in the imago Dei, not in spite of our impairments and contingencies, but through them."[51] She adds that diversity is important for the church as the body of Christ and is a hermeneutical key to understanding the Lord's Supper, such that "the church is impoverished without our presence."[52] She imagines a theology that opens the way for active agents to secure rights and access by means of self-assertion and resymbolization. She wants a level playing field, but is that enough for people with intellectual disabilities?

While Eiesland's work was groundbreaking in her affirmation of the full personhood of people with disabilities, her appropriation of a minority-group

---

[49]Tanner, *Christ the Key*, 40.
[50]McFarland, *Difference and Identity*, 10-11.
[51]Nancy L. Eiesland, *The Disabled God: Toward a Liberatory Theology of Disability* (Nashville: Abingdon, 1994), 101.
[52]Ibid., 115.

model for understanding disability, her liberation theology approach, and her close adherence to a strict social model of disability (wherein disability is primarily a social construction) makes her work less useful when considering the gifts and contributions of persons with intellectual disabilities. She does, however, bemoan the inattention given to other types of disabilities: "The paucity of theological exploration of social, emotional, and intellectual disabilities is scandalous."[53] Unfortunately, her theological anthropology does not provide a foundation for developing a theology of intellectual disability.

The best way to understand being human is not in terms of intrinsic faculties or capacity for self-determination. *Divine agency, not human agency, is at the center of our capacity to participate in the image of God to bear witness.* The idea of participating in God's mission is an essential element of a fully developed theological anthropology. As Paul Sands explains, "In a remarkable 'democratization' of the imago Dei concept, Genesis 1 indicates that all humans—not just rulers or other elites—are called to mediate God's presence, power, and rule in the earth."[54] God includes all creation in bearing the witness of the Spirit to the kingdom of God, and bearing witness is the special vocation of God's chosen people. But what are some ways that people with the particular challenges and limitations that accompany intellectual disabilities participate in congregational witness?

OUR ICONIC WITNESS: AN APPROPRIATION OF ORTHODOX THEOLOGIES OF MISSION AND EVANGELISM

Orthodox iconography can offer a helpful *sketch* (not a *prototype*—explained below) of evangelism and witness in relation to intellectual disabilities (ID). This sketch issues from my encounter with Orthodox iconography and my ten years of ministry to and with people with ID that I term "iconic witness." By suggesting the people with ID participate in the church's iconic witness, I am not proposing that people with disabilities are icons in the sense that they are burdened with the responsibility of pointing others to the divine or that they have a *special* endowed spiritual capacity so as to be "sacramental icons of heavenly life."[55]

---

[53]Ibid., 28.

[54]Sands, "Imago Dei as Vocation," 37.

[55]John Berkman, "Are Persons with Profound Intellectual Disabilities Sacramental Icons of Heavenly Life? Aquinas on Impairment," *Studies in Christian Ethics* 26, no. 1 (2013): 95.

The practice of iconography brings together the two themes with which this chapter is concerned: (1) theological anthropology and a vision of what it is to image God, and (2) an understanding of Christian witness that appreciates nonverbal and evocative responses. I believe the icon and the practice of iconography to inhere an understanding of Christian witness that relates well to intuitive, nonlinguistic ways of knowing. Attending to our iconic witness helps us appreciate the contributions of people with ID as indispensable and expands the possibilities for recognizing how everyone across the dis/ability spectrum participates in Christian witness.

Why do I call my iconic witness a sketch of evangelism and witness? Sketches and prototypes are, in this engagement, both ways of formulating theological concepts. According to Bill Buxton, computer scientist, designer, and the principal researcher for Microsoft Research, "Sketches dominate the early ideation stages, whereas prototypes are more concentrated at the later stages where things are converging within the design funnel."[56] Prototypes are didactic; they describe and refine, answer and test, attempt to resolve, and present specific depictions. Sketching, on the other hand, is intended to be evocative and suggestive. Sketches explore possibilities and question current practice; they propose and provoke, and they are tentative and non-committal.[57] I encourage you to play along, and perhaps you will move us further along the design funnel, where an increasing level of definition and explication become necessary. At this point we are simply sketching, and I hope you will partner with me and remember "without play imagination dies."[58] Like all theology, sketches are social devices that represent a shared awareness and require collaboration and community feedback in order to move forward.

In the practice of iconography, the writer (the one who paints the icon) proclaims or writes the gospel in color, line, and dimension. By means of the gilding, the postures of the people in the icon, the inverse perspective of the scene, and the sanctifying prayers that recognize the sacramental possibilities of the icon, the observer engaging the icon is drawn into

---

[56]Bill Buxton, *Sketching User Experiences: Getting the Design Right and the Right Design* (San Francisco: Morgan Kaufmann, 2007), 139.

[57]Ibid., 141.

[58]Ibid., 263.

communion with what is depicted and given a glimpse into the "good life" of the kingdom. To many Western viewers, the images seem odd—they seem to lack realism; they are flat and fail to represent three dimensions. Those represented in the icons do not have the expected proportions, and the icons include unfamiliar gestures, words, and symbols. The iconographers are not concerned with such critiques. They are remaining faithful to the sacred prototype and simply following the canons that govern the practice of iconography, since those practices have been established to ensure that what is most important is not lost. Ultimately, icons "express visually theological truths" and "incarnate a spiritual presence."[59] The iconographer's expectation is that in the encounter with an icon, the many things of this world that compete for our contemplation and devotion will be reoriented as we are guided and influenced by a vision of *theōsis*—a gospel affirmation and a witness to the fact that God was made human so that humanity can participate in God's divine life.

Icons can enlighten our understanding about what it means to participate in the witness of God. In exploring the iconic witness of the Orthodox tradition, I recognize that there is not one monolithic Orthodox tradition; Orthodoxy is a multicultural and variegated tradition. Nonetheless, I am convinced that the theology of the icon may inform our understanding of the image of God and rescue it from being dominated by notions of rationality. At the same time, icons can stimulate our attentiveness to mystery and create conceptual spaces where the church can appreciate some of the ways that people with ID participate in bearing the Spirit's witness. The power of the icon's witness comes from the Spirit of God and from the various elements used in the icon's composition (chalk, egg yolk, minerals, wood, and many other natural elements) being replaced in right relation to each other before God. If God is our iconographer, then each person—with their unique lines, textures, gestures, colors, capacities, and impairments—when called to the service of the Spirit is able to contribute to the iconic witness of the church. The iconic witness emphasizes the power of the Spirit—recall the earlier discussion on the importance of the Holy Spirit in Christian witness in chapter two—and strategic replacement over rational capacity, purposive

---

[59]Michel Quenot, *The Icon: Window on the Kingdom* (New York: St. Vladimir's Seminary Press, 1971), 93.

agency, moral responsibility, or a capacity for creativity. To hold an iconic understanding of witness is to acknowledge that the absence of people with intellectual disabilities from congregational ministry and witness diminishes the fitness of our witness.

ELEMENTS OF AN ICONIC WITNESS

The uncreated light. The transformative power of iconic witness is represented by an uncreated light. Light in icons does not seem to originate from an external source but instead emanates from the spiritually transformed person being depicted. Gilding, or the application of gold leaf to the image, is the convention used to express the eternal or uncreated light of God and the reality of transformation for those who are united with God. The light, as evidence of the divine life, is represented by the gold nimbus or halo that surrounds the head of the saint (sanctified person).

The creation of the halo by the iconographer is a delicate and theologically rich process. Having already prepared the wooden panel with gesso and animal glue, and having sketched the image, the iconographer lays down layers of clay (bole) where the gold leaf will be applied. The bole is prepared to receive the gold leaf through a long and involved process of sanding and burnishing. Unless the bole is prepared in this way, it will not be able to receive the gold. Once the bole/clay (which represents the earth creature—אָדָם, "Adam") is ready to receive the gold leaf (which represents the uncreated light and the sanctity of God), they are fused together by the warm, moist breath (רוּחַ, *ruach*—"breath, Spirit") of the iconographer as she breathes the gold leaf onto the bole, activating the animal glue.[60]

The process of icon writing and the icon itself reminds us that we bear the light of another and, in order to do this in a way that is faithful to the Spirit of God, are often submitted to a long and often uncomfortable process of preparation and formation.[61] The practice of iconography is a reminder that we bear the great treasure of the divine light on a vessel or backdrop of clay. The potential to bear this treasure or witness has less to do with our capacities, capabilities, or competencies than it does our strategic placement, formation, and reformation by God and the breath of the Spirit. To bear the divine light is a gift of grace to the community of faith and to a watching world. No one is impaired such that they can't be clay, and no single person should be disabled from participating in the church's witness because they aren't afforded a place in the congregation. An iconic witness recognizes that all of God's creation can bear the witness of the Spirit.

The uncreated light of the icon speaks to conversion and transformation. The saints depicted in the icons have reached *theōsis*; they share in the transfigured world brought about by Christ, and they call us to do the same. At the same time, they don't lose their personal identity in their union with God. Egg yolk combined with powdered pigment is mixed with water and vinegar, or wine. This makes the paint used to write the image of Christ on a wooden panel covered with gesso and animal glue. Yet the icon of Christ remains wood, pigment, and glue even as it performs a mediating function. Similarly, our evangelistic words remain words, our evangelistic activity remains human activity, and our witness remains human witness. Nevertheless we mediate Christ's presence and bear

---

[60]My knowledge of the process of creating icons comes from interviews with iconographer Don Merkley of St. Luke's Icon Guild, Williamsburg, Virginia, and from several books on the subject, including Mary Jane Miller, *Icon Painting Technique: A Meditative Guide to Egg Tempera Painting* (lulu.com, 2013), as well as Betsy Porter's website, www.betsyporter.com.

[61]"Like the Gospel texts, icons aim to transform the viewer," Jim Forrest explains. "We were made in the image and likeness of God, but the image has been damaged and the likeness all but lost. Since Adam and Eve, only in Jesus Christ were those attributes fully intact. The icon shows the recovery of wholeness." Jim Forrest, *Praying with Icons* (Maryknoll, NY: Orbis, 2008), 21.

witness to him, and communicate God's grace by the power of the Spirit.[62] Through our iconic witness, we are vessels of the divine, used by the Spirit, but we still use our gifts and maintain our identity. To return to the illustration from the opening pages, Megan, my friend from Friendship House, did not transcend her intellectual disability when she bore witness of the love of God to Seth—God used all God made Megan to be by nature and by grace.

Christocentric. An icon is not meant to stand alone—it stands in relationship to other icons and is oriented with them around Christ. Indeed, Jesus Christ is the true icon (Col 1:15), and we (together) are what Kallistos Ware terms "icons of the Icon" as we participate in Christ.[63] The icons are "motionless or frozen in postures of veneration, prophets, apostles and saints surround Christ, the 'living stone.'"[64] Individual lives and narratives are submitted to a communal vision that has as its focal point Jesus Christ, *Pantocrator*. From the Greek, *Pantocrator* translates "almighty" or "ruler of all." As an icon, the Christ Pantocrator icon occupies the central position in front

---

[62]Artist Egon Sendler explains, "In the icon we see a divine reality which goes beyond the dimensions of this earthly world but which at the same time respects this earthly world because it is created by God to become transfigured in his Spirit." Egon Sendler, *The Icon: Image of the Invisible: Elements of Theology, Aesthetics, and Technique* (Redondo Beach, CA: Oakwood, 1988), 182.

[63]Kallistos Ware, "Praying with Icons," in *One in 2000? Towards Catholic-Orthodox Unity, Agreed Statements and Parish Papers*, ed. Paul McPartlan (Slough, UK: St. Pauls, 1993), 162.

[64]Eugene N. Trubetskoi, *Theology in Color* (New York: St. Vladimir's Seminary Press, 1973), 25.

of the church, often inside the dome, and orients, both physically and theologically, all other icons.[65]

Jesus Christ, and the reality of the presence of Christ experienced through
the liturgy, is the central message of the church and serves as a catalyst for
mission. As Ion Bria explains of Orthodox mission theology,

> The knowledge of truth is given in the encounter with Jesus Christ, the per-
> sonal icon of the invisible God, manifested in human form and history, to
> create a reconciled humanity through his cross. . . . The centrality of Christ is
> fundamental because it obliges us to associate the church not only with that
> "great mystery" (Eph. 5:32) in which Christ invites to himself all those whom
> God has chosen, but also with the concrete realization of the Christian com-
> munity at Pentecost, and the eschatological reality of the body of Christ. The
> form of this continuous history is the building up of the church growing to-
> wards the fullness of Christ (evangelism and conversion continues with cat-
> echesis, education and formation of various ministries).[66]

Encounters with Christ rely on the initiative of God and not human initiative or capacities. And encounters with Christ issue in a concrete community. As people with ID take rightful places in the body of Christ, the
church grows toward the fullness of Christ.[67]

CHALLENGING OUR DEPENDENCE ON WORDS
AND RATIONAL CONCEPTS

Icons present the gospel in images rather than in words and abstract concepts. Art historian Nicholas Gendle has expressed it this way: "The icon *is*
the gospel in line and color, just as the sacred Scriptures communicate the

---

[65]"We have come to the central idea of all Russian icon painting. As we have seen, it subordinated
all the separate creatures—men, angels, animals—and even the world of plants—to the *common*
architectural design: what we have here is the *communality* of creatures within the church. But
the church holds them together not by walls or architectural lines: the unity of the church is not
imposed from the outside; it is a living whole, drawn together by the Spirit of love. The unity of
this church architecture comes from the new center of life, around which all creation gathers
and itself becomes the church of God [or the icon, as the church is the icon]. Because it gathers
around Christ . . . and it is the image of Christ that gives all this painting and architecture its
central meaning. The creatures gather in his name, and their union represents the *kingdom of
Christ* united from within." Ibid., 32.
[66]Ion Bria, "Orthodoxy and Mission," *International Review of Mission* 89, no. 352 (January 2000): 53.
[67]James Stamoolis quotes Anastasios Yannoulatos (favorably quoting Edwin D. Roels), "Christ is
 'the rallying point of the restored unity, the reintegrating center of human and cosmic life'"; see
James J. Stamoolis, *Eastern Orthodox Mission Theology Today* (Maryknoll, NY: Orbis, 1986), 51.

same truth in words."[68] Protestants have experienced a historic tension with icons. Many have been hesitant to embrace them and are especially uncomfortable with Orthodox theology that places icons on equal revelatory footing with Scripture. Nonetheless, I believe Protestants can learn more about their own traditions of evangelism and witness by considering the theology of iconography. Icons can remind Protestants both to relativize words and abstract theological concepts and to destigmatize experience and encounter so that we might be opened to confronting and affirming "an ineffable contact with God beyond words and concepts."[69] Our words reach and stretch but, like all other mediums of communication, are limited in their capacity to describe and bring us before the reality of God. Iconographers do not deny the value of words and concepts but instead attempt to extend beyond the capacity of words to convey a sense of being connected. Leonid Ouspensky and Vladimir Lossky explain it well in a segment of their standard work, *The Meaning of Icons*, that deserves to be quoted extensively:

> Christianity is the revelation not only of the Word of God but also of the Image of God, in which His Likeness is revealed. This godlike image is the distinctive feature of the New Testament, being the visible witness of the deification of man. The ways of iconography, as means of expressing what regards the Deity are here the same as the ways of theology. The task of both alike is to express that which cannot be expressed by human means, since such expression will always be imperfect and insufficient. There are no words, nor colors, nor lines, which could represent the kingdom of God as we represent and describe our world. Both theology and iconography are faced with a problem which is absolutely insoluble—to express by means belonging to the created world that which is infinitely above the creature. On this plane there are no successes, for the subject itself is beyond comprehension and no matter how lofty in content and beautiful an icon may be it cannot be perfect, just as no word image can be perfect. In this case, both theology and iconography are always a failure; for this value results from the fact that both theology and iconography reach the limit of human possibilities and prove insufficient. Therefore the methods used by iconography for pointing to the

---

[68]Nicholas Gendle, "Windows of Eternity: The Theology of Icons," in *Sacred Doorways: A Beginner's Guide to Icons,* ed. Linette Martin (Brewster, MA: Paraclete, 2002), 233.

[69]Ambrosios Giakalis, *Images of the Divine: The Theology of Icons at the Seventh Ecumenical Council,* ed. Robert J. Bast, Studies in the History of Christian Traditions (Leiden: Brill, 2005), 60.

Kingdom of God can only be figurative, symbolical, like the language of the parables in the Holy Scripture.[70]

Thus, "Divine truth lies beyond the capacity of the human intellect," Giakalis explains, "even at those times when God makes himself known to us through his uncreated energies, which although within our reach and capable of being experienced, nevertheless elude our understanding."[71] Ultimately, icons "express visually theological truths to incarnate a spiritual presence."[72] Icons remind us that the church's doctrinal teaching is supplemented and enlivened by participatory knowledge. They help us to remember the call of the Psalms that the invitation of the gospel is not only to hear and believe (Rom 10:4-17) but to taste and see (Ps 34:8). We are both a letter written from Christ (2 Cor 3:3) and the aroma or fragrance of Christ (2 Cor 2:15). "The Christian proclamation does not aim simply at persuading the intellect," explains Giakalis, "but much more, at assuring the heart 'by grace,' providing it with the saving and sanctifying experience of the 'unanimous' believing community."[73]

People with intellectual disabilities expose the limitations of our words for conveying truth. They remind the church that truth is "not as a product of the mind" but "a 'visit' and a 'dwelling' of an eschatological reality entering history to open it up as a communion-event."[74] The goal of our iconic evangelism is, ultimately, communion with those to whom we are bearing witness—and that communion is in Christ.

Advocates of Orthodox witness and evangelism seem to understand, or at least to foreground more than theologians from many other traditions, that minds are moved by affections, desire, and love. The Orthodox liturgy also invokes a heart language that transcends concepts and intellectual limitations: "The liturgy shows that the mystery of Christ and the truth of the good news are beyond our concepts and creeds. The most appropriate way

---

[70]Leonid Ouspensky and Vladimir Lossky, *The Meaning of Icons* (Crestwood, NY: St. Vladimir's Seminary Press, 1989), 48-49.

[71]Giakalis, *Images of the Divine*, 51.

[72]Michel Quenot, *The Icon: Window on the Kingdom* (New York: St. Vladimir's Seminary Press, 1971), 93.

[73]Giakalis, *Images of the Divine*, 53.

[74]John D. Zizioulas, *Being as Communion: Studies in Personhood and the Church* (Crestwood, NY: St. Vladimir's Seminary Press, 1997), 100.

to experience and communicate the message is to celebrate the faith through doxological hymns and prayers and sacramental symbolism."[75]

To put these Orthodox instincts in the language of someone closer to my own theological tradition, I will connect them to James K. A. Smith's reflection on Christian formation. Smith contends that the limitations and possibilities of Christian education can be applied to Christian witness and evangelism as well. He maintains that Christian education has typically been about communicating Christian ideas and information or even a Christian worldview (defined as a system of beliefs, ideas, and doctrines through which we interpret the world in a primarily cognitive, cerebral way). He challenges the conceptual category of "worldview" as being inattentive to our primary way of knowing, which is embodied and participatory. The notion of worldview paints a rationalist picture of the human and focuses on ideas and beliefs. Worldview conceives of people as primarily "thinking things" or cognitive machines or "containers for ideas." As Smith explains, "Our thinking and cognition arise from a more fundamental precognitive orientation to the world," specifically what we notice, value, and *love*. He continues, "liturgies—whether 'sacred' or 'secular'—shape and constitute our identities by forming our ultimate desires and our most basic attunement to the world. In short, liturgies make us certain kinds of people, and what defines us is what we *love*."[76]

The shopping mall offers a kind of iconic witness, but the vision of the good life is drastically different and very often at odds with the vision offered in the church. In the iconic witness of the mall we see "three-dimensional icons adorned in garb that—as with all iconography—inspires us to be imitators of these exemplars." They embody for us visions of the good life in tangible, replicable, and concrete ways. Smith explains, "Here is a religious proclamation that does not traffic in abstracted ideals or rules or doctrines, but rather offers to the imagination pictures and statues and moving images."[77] The mall is not a religiously neutral site, and the iconic witness of the mall is an effective evangelist for consumerism and excess in a way

[75]Ion Bria, *The Liturgy After the Liturgy: Mission and Witness in Orthodox Perspective* (Geneva: WCC Publications, 1996), 9.

[76]James K. A. Smith, *Desiring the Kingdom: Worship, Worldview, and Cultural Formation* (Grand Rapids: Baker Academic, 2009), 28 and 25.

[77]Ibid., 21.

that people can "taste and see." The church needs to examine the visions of the good life, or human flourishing, that are embedded in the broader American culture and that form us in particular ways though our partici- pation in cultural practices, and the church needs to be more attentive to its own practices that make up its iconic witness.

My point can perhaps be better comprehended by offering an example. In the Russian Orthodox tradition, the church is representative and reflective of the heavenly kingdom. From the beginning of Christianity in Russia, par- ticularly with the conversion of Vladimir the Great (Sviatoslavich), prince of Kiev, in 988, the church has played an essential part in witness and evan- gelism. Take, for example, the account of *The Russian Primary Chronicle.* After Bulgars, Germans, and Jews came before Vladimir to urge him to accept their faith, the Greeks appeared and encouraged the prince to send a group to experience how each group worshiped God and then make a decision. When the envoys returned to Russia having experienced worship with each group, they gave unfavorable reports of Bulgars, Germans, and Jews, but of the Greeks they said, "We knew not whether we were in heaven or on earth. For on earth there is no such splendor or such beauty, and we are at a loss to describe it. We only know that God dwells there among men . . . for we cannot forget that beauty." Following this report, Vladimir inquired where they should all receive baptism.[78] The beauty of the church participated in the witness of God by offering a vision of the beauty of the kingdom of God. Icons, as part of the church's witness, participate in that beauty, not by repre- senting saints with photo-like precision, but instead by giving a vision of *theōsis*, a vision of the "good life" according to the gospel.

How do we invite people to "taste and see" that the Lord is good? This is not the language of information, reason, ideas, and doctrine—it is the lan- guage of experience and participation. As I have maintained elsewhere, evangelism with people with intellectual disabilities should be practice cen- tered, because Christian practices form people at a level deeper than the intellect and have the flexibility and depth to connect with people of all ca- pacities.[79] Smith also argues for practice-centered ministry: "Christian

[78]Robert A. Hunt, "The Russian Primary Chronicle," in *The Gospel Among the Nations: A Docu- mentary History of Inculturation* (Maryknoll, NY: Orbis, 2014), 49-50.
[79]This is the thesis of my *Amplifying Our Witness*.

education shapes us, forms us, molds us to be a certain kind of people whose hearts and passions and desires are aimed at the kingdom of God. And that will require sustained attention to the practices that effect such transformation."[80] What intellectual capacities are needed for someone to bear or receive the hospitable presence of Christ, or participate in community of prayer, or receive the gift of friendship, or participate in the church's practice of testimony by bearing the witness of the Spirit?

Window to the kingdom. Another way that icons transcend reason is that they can provide, by the Spirit, a sense of being connected to the divine. Icons have been described as a window into the history and theology of the Orthodox Church and, according to Orthodox priest and professor of dogmatic theology Boris Bobrinskoy, they are much more—icons also serve as "a portal open to the glory and beauty promised to us, a grandeur and beauty

of which we receive a foretaste within the living experience of the church."[81] Russian Orthodox theologian Sergei Bulgakov contends that the "sacramental dimension of the icon is found not in its artistic expression but in the 'consecration that gives it its peculiar power to communicate with the beholder.'"[82] The icon, in this sense, serves as a window into the kingdom of heaven. An icon grants an invitation to be connected to a community of faith that includes those who have gone before us.

---

[80]Smith, *Desiring the Kingdom*, 18.
[81]Bobrinskoy, quoted in Quenot, *Icon*, 7.
[82]Quoted in Eric Lionel Mascall, *Theology and Images* (London: A. R. Mowbray, 1963), 43.

An iconic witness is not, therefore, a lonely account of the reality of God or an individualistic plea to convert. Instead, an iconic witness recognizes that we mediate a presence and take part in a tradition that gives an account of what could be described as an intuitive sense of being connected. According to artist Egon Sendler, "The icon is intended to be an image of the invisible and even the presence of the Invisible One." The icon is not to be reduced to a piece of inspiring artwork; the icon "becomes a link between the person represented and the person looking at the image."[83] Bishop Kallistos Ware describes his experience of entering a sparsely filled church in the following way: "I became aware of a presence—the presence of icons on the walls and on the icon-screen; and not only of that, but of the presence, mediated through these icons, of countless unseen worshippers. I felt that the church was not empty but full."[84] Our witness is an invitation to be connected, and being connected does not require any special abilities.

Invite and announce. One of the oldest icon types is the *Hodrigitria*, or "she who shows the way." This image is of Mary holding Jesus and motioning to him, pointing beyond herself to the one who gives life. Tradition holds that St. Luke was the first to write this icon, and there is, in fact, an icon of Luke painting the *Hodigritria*. One could claim that Luke's Gospel is a *Hodigritria* in words as he portrays Mary consistently pointing to her son.[85] The iconic way of witness humbly directs those we encounter to Jesus. Icons pose an invitation to join in a spiritual passage to *theōsis*. The iconic witness does not speak, but it is never mute—even when the witness seems less active and intentional and more evocative, the iconic witness calls people to encounter Jesus. What intellectual capacities are required to announce and invite in this way? Isn't this what Megan did?[86]

Megan overflows with a sense of belonging that is evangelistic in its expression, though she has neither the language nor the theological categories to articulate her faith. Still, she is able to invite others to join in that which

---

[83]Egon Sendler, *The Icon: Image of the Invisible: Elements of Theology, Aesthetics, and Technique* (Redondo Beach, CA: Oakwood, 1988), 39.

[84]Ware, *Praying with Icons*, 142.

[85]"In the Hodegitria icon, the Virgin is a guide who directs our attention away from herself; it is the iconic representation of her words at the wedding in Cana, 'do whatever he tells you.'" Linette Martin, *Sacred Doorways: A Beginner's Guide to Icon* (Brewster, MA: Paraclete Press, 2002), 169.

[86]See the introduction to this book.

she has experienced, that which gives her joy and contributes to her flourishing. Perhaps at the heart of her evangelism is the dictum *lex orandi, lex credendi* (translated "the law of praying is the law of believing," the phrase can mean that our worship, prayer, and actions reveal our beliefs)—perhaps she communicates her beliefs in her lived life of prayer.

Liturgical and congregational. Many iconographers contend that icons, in order to fulfill their mediating function and be something beyond inspirational artwork, cannot be separated from the rest of the tradition (the sacred texts, theology, architecture, other icons properly oriented, hymnody, and liturgy). Icons are only one part of what Edward Rommen terms "the core invitational context" of evangelism, by which he means the missional/liturgical life of the church.[87] When people step into an Orthodox church,

---

[87]Edward Rommen, *Come and See: An Eastern Orthodox Perspective on Contextualization* (Pasadena, CA: William Carey Library, 2013), 194-96.

they are swallowed up by the stories that are inscribed on the architecture and the elements of worship.

Evangelism and witness are ecclesial and liturgical in that they flow from and find their final meaning in the community's worship. The congregation, as the body of Christ and the community of people called to bear witness, offers a kind of "hermeneutic of the gospel"—a setting that offers a more complete account of God's redemptive work in the world than a disembodied (i.e., apart from the body of Christ) message.

There is an iconic aspect to the church's correspondence in God's self-witness in Christ. There is a sense in which the church is more than just an instrument conveying truths about life in Christ; it is a real sign and fore-taste of the kingdom of God. (Recall that this is Newbigin's common phrasing for how the congregation bears witness to the kingdom of God.) At the same time, there must be an "extension of the liturgical celebration into the daily life of the faithful in the world" or the "liturgy after the Liturgy."[88] As Ion Bria has suggested, the liturgy "calls and sends the faithful to celebrate the sacrament of the brother outside the temple in the public marketplace, where the cries of the poor and marginalized are heard."[89] The

---

[88]Ion Bria, "The Liturgy After the Liturgy," in *Orthodox Perspectives on Mission*, ed. Petros Vassiliadis, Regnum Edinburgh Centenary Series 17 (Oxford: Regnum Books International, 2013), 47.
[89]Ibid.

liturgy is not a mere centripetal instrument of proclamation. Instead, the "liturgy after the Liturgy" propels the congregation into the world, having been fed on the "pilgrim bread" of the Eucharist or Lord's Supper, to live supported by the company of the saints, scattered in the world according to the kingdom of God—to live into the calling of *theōsis* that they see represented in the icons. To be more specific, the liturgy after the Liturgy involves "a continuous liberation from the powers of the evil that are working inside us, a continual reorientation and openness to insights and efforts aimed at liberating human persons from all demonic structures of injustices, agony, loneliness, and at creating real communion of persons in love."[90]

The missionary calling of liberating people with ID from "injustices, agony, loneliness" is an important liturgical emphasis, not only for the sake of shalom today, but because many people with ID will come from the north, south, east, and west to "eat in the kingdom of God" (Lk 13:29) or be called in from the "streets and lanes of the town" to share in the great banquet of the Lord (Lk 14:21).

Cosmic in scope and honors creation. Many evangelical mission strategies emphasize the individual consequences of the fall and human separation from God as a way of motivating people to accept the gospel of salvation. An iconic witness offers creation as the orienting motif for mission with *theōsis* as the goal. *Theōsis* speaks to the mystical connection between creature and creator. Sin is thought of in terms of the icon losing its radiance; it is as though soot darkens the image rather than completely covering it. Jesus' death and resurrection reinstates the image so that in iconic evangelism and witness, the conversation is less about strategies and programs and more about practicing faith and participating in the life of God. In Protestant circles this approach has been termed *incarnational*— a touchpoint between God and creation that provides a model for mission and evangelism.

There are some difficulties with the incarnational conceptualization, for instance, using the incarnation as a model and attempting to become one with a "target" group as Christ became one with humanity; imagining our incomplete expression of the gospel is the one that needs to be incarnated

---

[90]Ion Bria, ed., *Martyria/Mission: The Witness of the Orthodox Churches Today* (Geneva: CWME/ WCC, 1980), 67.

into another setting; seeing our own presence as inherently redemptive and calling people to follow us; and grounding a ministry model in the unique act of God taking on humanity instead of grounding embodied, relational ministry in our common participation in Christ.[91] Still, one could properly term iconic witness "incarnational" and avoid the pitfalls of some other uses of the term because icons affirm the historicity and humanity of Jesus Christ. Irenaeus famously stated that if the Word of God became incarnate, it was so humankind might be deified: "The Word of God, our Lord Jesus Christ, who did, through His transcendent love, become what we are, that He might bring us to be even what He is Himself."[92] The icon of Christ does not merely show the divinity of Christ—it issues a summons, a call to participate in his life (a call to our own divinization) along with all of creation.

An appreciation for the cosmic scope of redemption is understated in Protestant theologies of evangelism and mission. Martin explains, "As a result of the incarnation, matter is no longer inert and warped but capable of mediating the immanent energies and uncreated light of the Creator."[93] Iconic witness represents the iconographer's response to God's call for all creation to participate in the act of witness and offers us a model of transformed lives that calls others to the possibility of their transformation. Michel Quenot, an Orthodox layman who is heavily invested in the history and theology of the icon, submits, "The materials used for making an icon are respected as God created them to be used from the mineral, plant organic world. They too are called to participate in the transfiguration of the cosmos, since the task of the iconographer is to spiritualize even our tangible reality."[94]

Orthodox theologian John Meyendorff clarifies that natural elements and human creativity work together in imaging God: "By sanctifying water, food, and plants, as well as the results of man's own creativity, such as works of art or technology . . . the Church replaces them all in their true relation, not only to God, but also to man, who is God's image."[95] God has chosen matter as a vehicle of the Spirit, and all God's creation can participate in this witness.

---

[91] Billings, *Union with Christ*, 123-65.
[92] Irenaeus, *Against Heresies* 5, pref., www.ccel.org/ccel/schaff/anfo1.ix.vii.i.html.
[93] Martin, *Sacred Doorways*, 236.
[94] Quenot, *Icon*, 83.
[95] John Meyendorff, *Byzantine Theology* (New York: Fordham University Press, 1974), 135.

In the icon and in our witness, "we see matter restored to harmony and so fulfilling its true vocation, which is to be theophanic, to reflect and transmit the divine glory."[96] An iconic witness includes an iconic vision of creation where "we can see each thing as a sacrament of the divine presence."[97] Iconic evangelism opens us up to being surprised by the ways that God's creation shares in the ministry of witness. It also demonstrates that the limits we tend to impose on those we might feel are incapable of participating in God's mission can be transcended. Bria, the most prolific Orthodox theologian of mission and evangelism, summarizes aptly, "The mission of the church is not created by Christians. God calls the church to surrender itself to Christ as his holy body, and has chosen his feeble sons and daughters to work through them for the salvation of us all."[98]

There is an implicit view in Orthodoxy that all of creation is called to participate in redemption. This includes plant and animal life as well as people of all backgrounds, ethnicities, cultures, physical abilities, and intellectual capacities. There is no more of a problem for a person with an intellectual disability participating in the iconic witness than there is someone with a doctoral degree in theology. In an iconic witness, the redemption of God is cosmic. In the icon, all of the elements are called together and strategically placed where they can bear witness. Evangelism is not a strategy to rescue an individual monad being saved from hell; it is a Spirit-enabled invitation to be a part of God's cosmos-wide redemption through Christ.

Mystery. People with intellectual disabilities awaken their congregations to the fact that much Protestant evangelism is more about manipulation than mystery. If the goal in evangelism and witness is to have people agree with certain statements about the faith or to recite a rote formula, then you may reach your goal without people ever encountering Christ. Bria goes so far as to declare, "Mission takes place where the mystery of God meets human history."[99]

Heather was at a Christian camp for young people with intellectual and developmental disabilities. She participated in adventurous activities that

---

[96]Ware, *Praying with Icons*, 160.
[97]Ibid., 161.
[98]Ion Bria, "Orthodoxy and Mission," *International Review of Mission* 89, no. 352 (January 2000): 50.
[99]Ibid., 54.

challenged her and deepened her friendships, and she saw the gospel lived out in the love her leaders and the staff demonstrated toward her. The typical routine at the camp included morning meetings, during which she sang songs with friends, laughed at entertaining skits, and heard a brief gospel message. The daily messages followed a format of gospel talks and offered a pattern for the expected response. The response was as easy as A-B-C: admit you are a sinner, believe in Christ, and commit your life to him. Invite Jesus into your heart. In order to give the campers the opportunity to process the message, campers returned to their cabins with their peers and leaders immediately after the meeting and were given the chance to write (or have a leader write for them based on their communication ability) a letter to God. Heather surprised everyone when she communicated her understanding of the gospel message. She wrote, "Thank you God for inviting me into your life"—a more faithful gospel than the one she received. This is not to say that a prayer prayed at camp following a series of messages that led to a scripted "A-B-C" response can't be a part of the mysterious work of Christ in drawing people to himself. Of course it can. I am simply critiquing such practices of evangelism as being disconnected from the larger practice of evangelism as viewed through the Orthodox iconic witness. Our Orthodox brothers and sisters teach that evangelism involves inviting someone into a kingdom and into the mysterious life of God that is experienced in this world through the community that bears the name of Christ, and this is something Protestants need to graft into our understandings of evangelism.

The Orthodox remind us that the gospel is not a manageable commodity, and our words, actions, and other presentations of the gospel cannot contain or exhaust its mystery. Iconic evangelism and witness invites people to union with something that they do not completely understand, and in the process of witness, everyone is changed. The icon speaks to a larger conversion—not simply a conversion of the mind but a complete transformation that comes through union with God and the mystery of transfiguration.

SUMMARY: OUR ICONIC WITNESS AND INTELLECTUAL DISABILITIES

A faithful Christian anthropology embraces the limitations and contingency of all human existence, and it recognizes that the image of God we bear is a gift expressed together in Christ and animated in us collectively by the Holy Spirit. People with intellectual disabilities are indispensable to their faith communities because among the other gifts and trials they offer, they remind their communities that our ability to image God is externally grounded. All personhood—able and disabled, in all its diversity—is grounded in gift, animated by the Spirit, and eschatological in nature. Stated succinctly, and borrowing Amos Yong's phrasing: "People with disabilities are created in the image of God that is measured according to the person of Christ" just like everyone else.[100]

Our iconic witness doesn't exclude anyone because it is not dependent on a strategy or capacity that is intrinsic to us. The witness we bear is a gift expressed through grace, the power of the Spirit, and divine replacement. The testifying powers of the iconic witness do not require intellectual capacities, physical abilities, or social skills. At the same time, our iconic witness appreciates and allows full expression for rational capacity, purposive agency, moral responsibility, and human creativity.

The only way that people with disabilities who are part of the body of Christ can fail to offer their contribution to the ministry and witness of the church in our iconic witness is if they are not afforded a place within Christian congregations. The absence of their concerns and presence in theological schools and congregations diminishes the church's capacity for ministry and the fitness of our witness. No one is impaired to the extent that they can't bear the witness of the Spirit, and no single person should be disabled from participating in the church's witness.

Until we understand that our light is a reflection and that our image bearing is derivative of the one true *eikōn* of God by the Spirit, we will struggle to find a place for disability studies in our seminaries, roles for people with disabilities in our churches, and space for people with disabilities as friends or in our homes. We simply will not value their gifts enough to act to change congregational policies, programs, theologies, and liturgies. When we recognize that our witness is an iconic witness and we need everyone in order to be complete, then we will begin to understand the indispensability of people with disabilities.

---

[100]Yong, *Bible, Disability, and the Church*, 13.

5
....

[Dis]abling Theological Education

THE PROBLEM

Lennard Davis claims in *Enforcing Normalcy*, which is part of the core canon in disability studies, that while even in progressive studies, "the main attractions of race, class, and gender continue to grab the attention of professors and students, as well as of the general public, the concept of disability is safely hidden on the sidelines away from much scrutiny."[1] Not surprisingly, then, while issues of class, race, ethnicity, and gender have been receiving increasing attention from seminaries and divinity schools, the human experience of disability rarely enters the theological imagination. Those who have made the case for disability to be included in discussions of multiculturalism and diversity have faced resistance. In the humanities, "Attempts to include . . . disability studies in curriculum transformation efforts have been welcomed by some, and criticized by others. Ironically, some of the critics are those who are the strongest proponents of diversifying the curriculum. However, their conceptualization of diversity does not included disability."[2] For our more theologically focused purposes, Robert C. Anderson, who headed the Center for Religion and Disability, maintains that disability is "the ultimate null curriculum in institutions of graduate theological education."[3] Information, concepts, ideas, theories, or models can be designated as part of a null curriculum when

---

[1]Lennard J. Davis, *Enforcing Normalcy: Disability, Deafness, and the Body* (New York: Verso, 1995), 158.
[2]Simi Linton, Susan Melo, and John O'Neill, "Disability Studies: Expanding the Parameters of Diversity," *The Radical Teacher* 47 (Fall 1995): 10.
[3]Robert C. Anderson, "In Search of the Disabled Human Body in Theological Education: Critical Perspectives on the Construction of Normalcy—An Overview," in *Graduate Theological Education and the Human Experience of Disability*, ed. Robert C. Anderson (New York: The Haworth Pastoral Press, 2004), 48.

they are ever addressed, which, of course, communicates something about their worth to the instructor. For example, Mary Hess and Stephen Brookfield expose how "racism" has impacted white students as a null curriculum.[4] In recent years, in response to cultural movements, this issue is being attended to more directly in seminaries. Communities of theological learning are discovering that directly addressing racism and privilege helps students to notice and engage, at various levels, the unjust systems that sustain privilege in ways that help them to be more sensitive and thoughtful ministers. Unfortunately, unlike issues of racism and white privilege, disability concerns remain in the null curriculum, marginally represented at best and absent in most theological schools. Perhaps this is because theological education has followed the academy, where, according to disability scholars Joseph Valente and Kathleen Collins, "schooling is about defining, locating, measuring, and remediating *ability*."[5]

In this chapter I will continue the previous project of [dis]abling. Chapter three [dis]abled mission history in the United States and demonstrated how evangelistic efforts and Deaf agency worked together to develop Deaf

---

[4]Mary Hess and Stephen Brookfield, *Teaching Reflectively in Theological Contexts: Promises and Contradictions* (Malabar, FL: Krieger, 2008), 165.

[5]Joseph Michael Valente and Kathleen Collins, "[Dis]Ableing Educational Inequalities: A Disability Studies in Education Perspective," *Review of Disability Studies: An International Journal* 12, no. 1 (2015): 1.

culture and a Deaf theological voice that can provide insight for comprehending and practicing congregational witness. Chapter four [dis]abled
theological anthropology and evangelism by considering insights that can
be gained from the ways people with intellectual disabilities inhabit the
world. This chapter addresses one of the fountainheads of congregational
leadership and theological education, and imagines ways that we can
[dis]able theological education for the sake of enabling a more credible and
faithful witness to the gospel.

The task of evaluating the faithfulness and effectiveness of theological
education can be guided by practical theology. According to John Swinton
and Harriet Mowat, "Practical Theology is critical, theological reflection on
the practices of the Church as they interact with the practices of the world,
with a view to ensuring and enabling faithful participation in God's redemptive practices in, to and for the world."[6] Practical theology is a field that
has been reflecting on and refining ministerial formation for years. In the
past forty years, the field has been challenging the direction of the entire
enterprise of theological education.

Edward Farley's classic critique of seminaries was that they operated
within a "clerical paradigm," and Bonnie Miller-McLemore's nuancing of
Farley's appraisal cast theological education as operating within an "academic paradigm." To these evaluations, we can add that seminaries have
unintentionally embraced and perpetuated an ableist paradigm that has
serious consequences for the spiritual and ministerial formation that
happens in classrooms, on campuses, online, and in churches.[7]

Farley believes that seminaries have moved from engaging "theology's
primary genre," which is the encounter of and response to God, and settled
for passing on abstract and impersonal knowledge about the Christian faith
along with the skill necessary for executing the tasks associated with being
a professional minister. He suggests that as long as theology's primary
setting is in an academy, then theology will continue to be reduced and

---

[6]John Swinton and Harriet Mowat, *Practical Theology and Qualitative Research* (London: SCM
Press, 2006), 6.

[7]Edward Farley, *Practicing Gospel: Unconventional Thoughts on the Church's Ministry* (Louisville:
Westminster John Knox, 2003), and Bonnie J. Miller-McLemore, "The Clerical Paradigm: A
Fallacy of Misplaced Concreteness?," *International Journal of Practical Theology* 11, no. 3 (2007):
19-38.

restricted to methods and techniques of clergy education. Miller-McLemore contends that the principal issue with this kind of ministerial preparation is not that it is too clerical but that it is too academic. Theology, as a result, becomes the responsibility of credentialed academicians, is written in increasingly technical language, and is directed toward an audience that is removed from the Christian life and ministry of the laity. Both Farley and Miller-McLemore raise significant issues with the content and shape of theological education, but Anderson adds that there are deeper, even more foundational problems with our system—whether too clerical or overly professional, it is exclusive in a more profound and disturbing way. People with disabilities are at best marginalized in theological education, and the "frame of reference for educational structures is an able-bodied one."[8]

What makes the relative absence of people with disabilities and the scantiness of disability interests being addressed in theological education so odd is the prevalence of disability in the United States. As described in the introductory chapter, people with disabilities can be conceived of as the largest multicultural minority group. Most people will likely enter this group at some point, either permanently or temporarily, against their will. If abstracted as a group, "the disabled" includes a collection of people who can be found in every class, race, ethnicity, and economic circumstance.

Theological schools have unwittingly perpetuated ableist and normate biases because these biases are embedded in the ways we organize and articulate Christian history, in the ways we practice and formulate theology, in our hermeneutical approaches to the Bible, in the ways that we imagine ministry and liturgy, in our community life and ways of relating to each other, and, finally, in what we consider a potentially successful student in such a system. A normate bias—or "normalcy," as Lennard Davis terms it—is an unacknowledged power that drives a society toward homogeneity and thus toward narrow conceptions of humanness, embodiment, health, and community.[9] The "normate" is the composite (collective) identity position held by those who are not marginalized by a marked body or stigmatized identity (black, foreign, female, disabled). The normate is the imagined "every man" ("man" being used intentionally here) that is valued in American

---

[8]Anderson, "In Search of the Disabled Human Body," 38.
[9]Davis, *Enforcing Normalcy*, 23-49.

culture and that silences disability concerns. "As the norm becomes neutral in an environment created to accommodate it," explains Rosemarie Garland-Thomson, who coined the term *normate*, "disability becomes intense, extravagant, and problematic. Disability is the unorthodox become flesh, refusing to be normalized, or homogenized."[10]

Of course, theological institutions are not insulated cultures. While they can resist the values of the dominant culture at key points, they often perpetuate those values, which leads the theological community toward a reduced understanding of spiritual giftedness, ministry, and witness. Unfortunately, notions of ability and normality have become invisible assumptions in seminaries, and theological institutions have colonized disability concerns and perspectives into settled theological concepts. They have not allowed the lived experience of disability to challenge, unsettle, or enrich theological concepts and pastoral practice. Regrettably, seminaries and divinity schools have been extremely effective in discipling and forming students into an understanding that disability belongs to the null curriculum.

A Call to Action

For Christian seminaries preparing men and women to lead the church in mission,[11] thinking through disability concerns is vitally important because, as I have indicated to this point, the experience of disability is a common aspect of the human experience, and all people are called to participate in God's ongoing redemptive work in the world. A recent study by Erik Carter and Naomi Annandale, which included correspondence with representatives from 118 Association of Theological Schools (ATS) member institutions, found "the majority of respondents perceived that their graduates were *not at all* (3.4%) or *only a little* (70.7%) prepared to respond to spiritual and theological questions resulting from disability-related human experiences."[12] Because theological institutions have been

---

[10]Rosemarie Garland-Thomson, *Extraordinary Bodies: Figuring Disability in American Culture and Literature* (New York: Columbia University Press, 1997), 24.

[11]The mission statement of my seminary, Western Theological Seminary, is the following: "The purpose of Western Theological Seminary is to prepare Christians called by God to lead the church in mission" (www.westernsem.edu/about/mission-vision/).

[12]Naomi Annandale and Erik W. Carter, "Disability and Theological Education: A North American Study," *Theological Education* 48, no. 2 (2014): 92.

slow to address the reality of the experience of disability in any comprehensive way, and because there are few models for infusing theological
education with disability concerns, Carter and Annandale conclude their
study with the following plea: "While we acknowledge the very real com-
plexities associated with ensuring that theological schools prepare students for the myriad aspects of ministry they may undertake, we are convinced that the ubiquity of disability calls for much greater attention than
is currently provided."[13]

Theirs was not the first appeal to theological institutions to address the
experience of disability. In 1978, Harold Wilke urged ATS institutions to
make professional theological education more accessible. Born without
arms and considered the first modern theologian to deal directly with disability, Wilke saw access through the lens of both theology and civil rights
as both a moral and legal issue. He recommended changes in architecture
and attitude and encouraged theological schools to consider hosting symposia and teaching courses that would raise awareness about disability concerns.[14] In 2003, Robert C. Anderson made a case to ATS institutions for
broadening knowledge about the human experience of disability throughout
the graduate theological curriculum. He suggested a plan that would employ
a combination of methodologies for affecting change including hosting collaborative symposia and workshops; developing courses; offering training
for faculty, staff, and administration; funding research scholarships and
graduate assistantships; and offering continuing and distance education to
make sure practitioners have opportunities for growth.[15] In 2008, ATS responded by adopting a policy statement titled *Disability and Theological
Education*, in which they called on schools to "work toward the fullest possible inclusion of all God's people in their work and witness." The document
challenged ATS schools to "prepare men and women for ministry with attention to the unique gifts and needs of persons with disabilities who will

---

[13]Ibid., 94.
[14]Harold H. Wilke, "Access to Professional Education," *Theological Education* 15 (Autumn 1978):
18-32. Wilke was at the signing of the ADA and received a pen (with his foot) from President
Bush.
[15]Robert C. Anderson, "Infusing the Graduate Theological Curriculum with Education About
Disability: Addressing the Human Experience of Disability in the Theological Context," *Theological Education* 39, no. 1 (2003): 131-53.

be present in their congregations and communities."[16] One year earlier, the World Council of Churches (WCC) had encouraged schools to adopt courses such as "Introducing Disability Discourse for Theological and Ministerial Formation" and "Inclusive Community: Disability Perspectives." The purpose of such courses, they explained, would be to explore "new ways of embracing an inclusive understanding of the body of Christ by incorporating the experiences of disability and to introduce disability discourses in theological and ministerial formation in students and to equip them for holistic ministry."[17]

Carter and Annandale's recent findings suggest that the recommendations by the WCC and ATS have not been adopted. Very few seminaries have acted to take disability seriously as a theological and missiological issue. A Google search of the terms *disability* and *seminary* returns top results that indicate minimal engagement with disability: "disability concerns," "accommodations," "assistance," and "policy and procedures." For most seminaries, it appears *disability* is still primarily a term that designates issues of access and accommodation rather than an animating theological perspective.[18] In my searches and conversations with ATS administrators, I was unable to find any comprehensive program of disability and theology or disability and ministry housed in a seminary or divinity school. What has been offered in theological schools are occasional electives. Certainly it is the case that seminaries face some obstacles to infusing the curriculum with disability concerns. According to disability scholars Simi Linton, Susan Mello, and John O'Neill, obstacles to incorporating disability studies into higher education curriculums include:

1. low representation of people with disabilities in academic settings;

2. the assumption that disability studies has its own place in the curriculum;

---

[16]"Disability and Theological Education," The Association of Theological Schools, February 17, 2015, www.ats.edu/uploads/about-ats/documents/policy-guideline-disability-and-theological -education.pdf.

[17]*Ministerial Formation* 109 (July 2007): 66.

[18]According to special education professor Lauren Shallish, "There has been limited inquiry into disability apart from the administration of services and experience of accommodations provided by the offices of disability services." Lauren Shallish, "A Different Diversity? Challenging the Exclusion of Disability Studies from Higher Education Research and Practice," in *Disability as Diversity in Higher Education: Policies and Practices to Enhance Student Success*, ed. Eunyoung Kim and Katherine C. Aquino (New York: Routledge, 2017), 21.

3. the belief that a university is responsible only to provide services (relevant to the point I just made above with my Google search); and

4. conceptions of diversity that don't include disability.[19]

Seminaries and divinity schools face the same obstacles, yet the effort to overcome these obstacles to date has been embarrassingly minimal.

Returning to the recent study by Carter and Annandale, of 118 member institutions of ATS, a mere thirty schools indicated that they had offered any disability-related courses in the past three years, and only 72 percent had libraries that included disability resources.[20] The authors conclude,

> Our findings suggest a focus on people with disabilities often receives relatively limited attention within the theological curriculum. Relatively few leaders indicated that disability was addressed extensively in any of the six curricular areas. Although occasionally addressed in courses addressing pastoral care, religious education and spiritual formation, disability was less frequently addressed in the disciplines of theology, biblical studies, and preparation for ministry.[21]

The researchers continue by articulating their concern, justifiably I believe, that by limiting the scope of disability concerns to the pastoral ministries, seminaries might be communicating subtly that disability interests aren't relevant to history, theology, or biblical studies (again, the null curriculum).

In other words, in the seminary, disability concerns might be guided by the fields of special education or bioethics and find a home in religious education or pastoral care. However, disability rarely intersects with the theological heart of the institution in terms that challenge their theological tradition's capacity to answer the difficult questions that arise from the human experience of disability. The key finding in Carter and Annandale's study mentioned earlier in this chapter is worth repeating: out of 118 ATS institutions, nearly 75 percent perceive their graduates only minimally prepared to address issues raised by the human experience of disability if at all.[22]

---

[19]Linton, Mello, and O'Neill, "Disability Studies," 9-10.
[20]Annandale and Carter, "Disability and Theological Education," 90.
[21]Ibid., 92.
[22]Ibid.

The thesis of this book is that mission studies is uniquely equipped to engage disability in terms of gains to theology rather than in terms of individual deficiencies or obstacles to be overcome. Disability perspectives can offer insight to biblical interpretation, theology, and the practice of ministry, and the presence and perspectives of people with disabilities can add credibility and vibrancy to congregational witness. Seminaries and divinity schools could positively engage disability presence and perceptions in a way that renews and enriches the theological imagination. A more faithful witness to the kingdom of God will accompany our willingness to [dis]able theological education.

[Dis]abling our teaching will require including the presence of people with disabilities in our institutions: in leadership roles, as mentors, and as students so that the human experience of disability ceases to be abstracted. It also involves creating both intentional spaces in our curriculum for addressing issues related to disability and making disability concerns a dimension of the entire curriculum to reflect the reality that disability concerns are human concerns. These three themes—presence, intention, and dimension—are the scaffolding of my proposal for disabling theological education.

DISABLING THEOLOGICAL EDUCATION

In "[Dis]Abling Educational Inequalities," Joseph Valente and Kathleen Collins use insights and evaluative criteria from a subfield of disabilities studies known as disability studies in education to critique current educational theory and practice. They develop and apply a heuristic lens to educational practices and discourse that has the effect of [dis]abling, by which the authors mean, "These principles together can comprise a 'habit of mind' to position the [dis]abling researcher to counter assumptions about ability and disability."[23] This notion of [dis]abling envisions disability as a category of critical inquiry that provides insight into how seminaries, divinity schools, and other theological training centers could better prepare students for ministry and mission. The authors of *Disability Studies: Enabling the Humanities* explain the possibilities: [dis]abling "seeks to redress the exclusion of disability and disabled people from our critical discourses, our

---

[23]Valente and Collins, "[Dis]Ableing Educational Inequalities," 4.

scholarly imaginations, and our classrooms. It seeks to *enable* in the way that some of us in disability studies scholarship and activist work have attempted to reclaim enabling as a term of our own rather than one rooted in rehabilitation, social welfare, and medical discourses."[24]

The heuristic approach described above involves four moves: "defamiliarizing the familiar"; "destabilizing ability-normative constructs"; "identifying and disrupting neoliberal self-sufficiency myths"; and "locating the inclusion/exclusion of narratives shaping discourses." The authors apply their critical lens to the Race to the Top federal education reforms and expose underlying ableist assumptions and practices that they believe have deleterious effects for all students, especially students with disabilities. These four unsettling components of a [dis]abling lens can be applied similarly and with equal benefit to the curricular design and educational practices of theological institutions.

De-familiarize the familiar (complexify common sense). English professor and disability theorist Rosemarie Garland-Thomson, in her important work *Extraordinary Bodies*, de-familiarizes the notion of being "able-bodied," especially as a conceptual opposite of "disability," by demonstrating how both concepts are culturally constructed.[25] The conceptual category of disability becomes de-familiarized through a process of exposing unarticulated but powerful expectations and norms that reveal deeply held cultural assumptions about embodiment, power, pathology, and politics with which the concept is laden. These assumptions, when unexamined, are assumed to be neutral. Garland-Thomson explores these concepts in American culture through literature and demonstrates that they are not neutral but instead bear and perpetuate a "normate" bias that supports an understanding of superiority for the nondisabled, unmarked, and male. *Normate* designates the perspective or person that is defined and constructed as the normal and neutral center against the abnormal, marked, deviant, extraordinary, or disabled margins.[26]

Another way to de-familiarize the familiar is through the process of translation—the translation of texts into other languages, the translation of

---

[24]Sharon L. Snyder, Brenda Jo Brueggemann, and Rosemarie Garland-Thomson, eds., *Disability Studies: Enabling the Humanities* (New York: The Modern Language Association of America, 2002), 3.

[25]Garland-Thomson, *Extraordinary Bodies*, 6.

[26]Ibid., 8.

concepts across cultures, the translation of spoken English into sign language, or the translation of theological concepts into less-abstract modes that people with intellectual disabilities can understand. The process of translation disrupts and challenges commonsense meanings. Translation can "serve the purpose of disrupting the complacent belief that one understands one's own thoughts and the language in which one formulates one's thoughts. It can illustrate that ideas and concepts that seemed familiar and commonsensical carry foreign and unfamiliar traces that call into question their current obviousness."[27] Translation can be used to communicate meaning, but it also simultaneously unsettles meaning and creates the kind of space that is necessary to call the seemingly neutral and obvious into question.

De-stabilize ability-normative constructs. Rather than attempting to ignore the real issues related to the lived experience of disability represented in platitudinous and impotent phrases such as "we are all disabled" or "handi-capable," instead, we should acknowledge the ability-disability continuum that we all experience. We should communicate in words and actions that "able" is not equivalent to normal or the opposite of disabled. Having a disability, for many people, involves the experience of finding oneself on the continuum of abled-disabled at different times, to greater or lesser degrees, for lesser or greater periods, in episodic or permanent states, in some circumstances and not others. For those who find it difficult to move beyond the binaries of able-disabled, a crosscultural perspective, such as that of Ingstad and Whyte (introduced in chapter two), can be particularly helpful. They guide us toward contextual factors that inform our evaluations regarding what actually disables someone. Similarly, the authors of *Disability Studies: Enabling the Humanities* address dichotomies in language and practices that "determine or prescribe what it means to be an abled self in a particular context."[28]

Disrupt myths of self-sufficiency. A particularly difficult task for [dis]abling theology in the United States is addressing the myths of self-sufficiency. Despite a central Christian theological conviction that all people are saved

---

[27]Claudia Ruitenberg, "Distance and Defamiliarisation: Translation as Philosophical Method," *Journal of Philosophy of Education* 43, no. 3 (2009): 426.

[28]Snyder, Brueggemann, and Garland-Thomson, *Disability Studies*, 5.

by another and that all of the work that we do on behalf of God is Spirit enabled, the American notion of self-sufficiency still finds a comfortable home in theological higher education and in congregational discipleship. If anyone doubts these myths exist, consider how few people with disabilities have a PhD, are employed as professors at seminaries or divinity schools, are enrolled in graduate theological education, or pastor churches.[29] The problem of people with disabilities being underrepresented in the academy begins much earlier in undergraduate education. According to one study, 66 percent of students with disabilities in American colleges and universities do not persist to graduation, "a rate 17% higher than their peers without disabilities."[30] Why is this? Part of the problem is that students are moving from high school, where they are supported by IDEA and IEPs (educational statutes), to college, where they are supported by Section 504 of the Rehabilitation Act of 1973 and the ADA (civil rights statutes without a corresponding educational service requirement).[31] But of equal importance, myths of self-sufficiency limit our imagination regarding the possibilities of people with disabilities, and these myths "are used to frame what can and should be achieved by and with an individual with a disability."[32]

Dis-locate narratives. Much of this book has been an attempt to reshape our discourse about disability, mission, and witness by privileging "counternarratives, insider accounts, and experiential knowledge."[33] I have attempted to offer marginalized voices a place at the interpretive center of my understanding of mission history and theology. These voices provide distinctive and previously absent perspectives for understanding the church's theology of mission and fresh intonations to our witness to God's redemptive work in a world filled with dis/abilities. And, as Debbie Creamer explains, it is also a matter of justice:

---

[29]Joseph Grigely, "The Neglected Demographic: Faculty Members with Disabilities," *The Chronicle of Higher Education*, June 24, 2017, www.chronicle.com/article/The-Neglected-Demographic/240439.

[30]Allison R. Lombardi and Adam R. Lalor, "Faculty and Administrator Knowledge and Attitudes Regarding Disability," in Kim and Aquino, *Disability as Diversity in Higher Education*, 107.

[31]Wanda Hadley and D. Eric Archer, "College Students with Learning Disabilities: An At-Risk Population Absent from the Conversation of Diversity," in Kim and Aquino, *Disability as Diversity in Higher Education*, 78-79.

[32]Snyder, Brueggemann, and Garland-Thomson, *Disability Studies*, 5.

[33]Ibid.

The voices of people with disabilities have been historically excluded from theology and theological reflection. It is an issue of justice that we seek now to open ourselves and bring our marginalized voices to the center of theological discourse. Seeking out and inviting the stories and concerns and ideas of people with disabilities in an authentic way allows us to participate and respond faithfully to those who have been oppressed and outcast.[34]

Below are two examples of how I have seen these four dynamics at work [dis]abling our theological education at Western Theological Seminary for the sake of enabling witness.

EXAMPLES OF [DIS]ABLING

Amanda. Amanda, a young woman with Down syndrome who lives at Friendship House, has contributed to the transformation of theological education at Western Theological Seminary by enrolling in a Hebrew language course. Old Testament Professor Tom Boogaart has related how having Amanda in his class challenged his pedagogy, biblical hermeneutics, and theological imagination, and confirmed his idea that the spirit of a seminary classroom should be more collaborative than competitive.[35]

Boogaart had long been suspicious of the assumptions that guided theological education. The teaching model in which he was formed was hierarchical, celebrating the expertise of the instructor, who was understood to be the source of knowledge and the gatekeeper of competency. It was individualistic and encouraged personal achievement over communal commitment. It was informational trafficking in the transmission of facts and methods and not invested in forming the character of students. It was threatening to students because achievement in class was related to a complex of other issues, from maintaining a GPA to preserving a scholarship. In that environment, Boogaart felt that he couldn't foster the relationship with the Bible or theology that the church needs in order to flourish. Before he even met

---

[34]Deborah Creamer, "Toward a Theology That Includes the Human Experience of Disability," in Anderson, *Graduate Theological Education and the Human Experience of Disability,* 66.

[35]Much of this section is taken directly from Dr. Boogaart's presentation at The Summer Institute on Theology and Disability, Holland, Michigan, 2016, with his permission. It is interesting to note that Dr. Boogaart's approach is similar to what Christina Yuknis and Eric Bernstein propose in their "culturally relevant disability pedagogy." See Christina Yuknis and Eric R. Bernstein, "Supporting Students with Non-Disclosed Disabilities: A Collective and Humanizing Approach," in Kim and Aquino, *Disability as Diversity in Higher Education.*

Amanda, Boogaart had settled on three convictions that he believed would make his classes more inclusive of different learning styles and would make his class more spiritually formative: a classroom must be safe and foster trust among instructors and peers; a classroom must be playful, lively, open, and imaginative; and instruction needs to be embodied, touching on all the senses, which are "doors to the heart." Instructors were a part of the circle of learning and on the same level with students, physically and dispositionally, as fellow learners. Instructors negotiated with each student to set appropriate yet stretching goals for the course within the extents of their abilities. The introduction of Amanda to his Hebrew class would challenge the efficacy of his teaching practices and would test whether the environment was inclusive.

An enthusiastic participant with a contagious eagerness for learning, Amanda found that while she could participate in the class at a high level, some exercises were beyond her ability. When this was the case, sometimes her peers helped her. However, most of the class was conducted in a way that was accessible to her. For example, when introducing Hebrew vocabulary in the class, students first hear, then speak, and then read and enact the words. When students enacted imperatives in playful and embodied ways (sit, stand, come, etc.), Amanda determined the pace of the class. When Amanda was asked to stand on top of a desk to illustrate a word and required supports to stabilize her, her peers were learning more than Hebrew; they were learning to attend to each other, to care for each other, and to support one another. Amanda had an evocative witness in the classroom—her mere presence changed class dynamics. But she did much more than simply evoke.

In order to better learn the narratives of the Old Testament, students acted them out, and Amanda brought interpretive insight to the performance of the binding of Isaac (Gen 22:1-14). To perform any biblical account, students must imagine the objects in the account, tones of voice, sounds, body placements, and postures that convey emotions. All enactments are interpretative.[36] In the

---

[36]See David Rhoads, "Performance Criticism: An Emerging Methodology in Biblical Studies," Society of Biblical Literature, www.sbl-site.org/assets/pdfs/rhoads_performance.pdf. "Eventually, I no longer see words on a page or hear sounds in my head. Rather, I imagine the scenes in my mind and I tell/show what I 'see/hear' to a living audience before me. My students who learn texts for performance also speak of the enlivening of their imagination, a new capacity to identify with the different characters, and a fresh sense of the emotive dimensions of the text" (4).

performance of the account of the binding of Isaac, Amanda wanted to be the angel. During the presentation, when Abraham's knife was raised, Amanda, the angel, took the knife from Abraham, cradled it in her arms, and carried it off stage. In the biblical account, there is no explanation of what happened to the knife. Boogaart thought of the tradition in the Bible where violence is overcome: weapons are beaten into plowshares; the Ninevites lay down their weapons and turn to God; and Jesus commands his disciples to put away the sword. He had never thought that the story of Abraham and Isaac might be part of the larger narrative of what we are supposed to do with weapons and violence. Her insight was refreshing, and Boogaart witnesses to the fact that Amanda was among a group of students who formed a community where truths began to come alive through their relationships.

Once a class has experienced the presence of Amanda, once the gifts of a person with disabilities are infused in the life of a school, we are faced with a number of issues. How do we decide who belongs in our classrooms at a graduate theological school that has the primary purpose of forming people for ministry and mission? What criteria do we use to decide who is capable of learning? Test scores and GPA are the traditional criteria. It is true even for seminaries that "the frame of reference for educational structures is an able-bodied one."[37] But another vision for a community of learning is slowly emerging. Amanda's presence is helping to [dis]able theological education and is challenging WTS to reflect more deeply in all course offerings so Western can be "more like the community that Jesus desires it to be" (Boogaart).

Amanda's presence in class helped to de-familiarize pedagogy and invalidated widely accepted criteria for predetermining who can be a successful student. Additionally, the opportunity to be a student at WTS provided Amanda with a new identity, "Lila" (her name in the Hebrew class), and a new social role in the community (student), and those aspects of her identity needed to find support and affirmation throughout the campus after the course was completed. Amanda's presence in the Hebrew class destabilized dis/ability constructs because while full participation in the class was challenging for her, Amanda was able to be successful with supports.

---

[37] Anderson, "In Search of the Disabled Human Body," 38.

Additionally, she contributed to the interpretative community through her artwork, her affect, and her interpretations. Amanda's presence in Hebrew class disrupted myths of self-sufficiency by making it acceptable for all students to ask for help. She exposed cultural norms of individualism and competitiveness that can undermine the explicit theological teaching at a seminary. Finally, Amanda's presence in the Hebrew class, and the account of her involvement, has become part of WTS's story. Students no longer face the "null curriculum" of disability because disability has a face on campus. And because disability has a face on campus, it has a voice in hermeneutics, theology, and the way we envision and execute ministerial practices.

Randy Smit. Randy Smit is an author, poet, artist, theologian, and student peer group leader at Western Theological Seminary, and founder and director of Compassionate Connection. He also has spinal muscular atrophy. Randy is a valued and respected ally of the Formation for Ministry team at WTS who makes a positive impact on our learning community.

Randy's presence at WTS de-familiarizes the concept of a leader. Although we are all contingent and vulnerable, Randy leads with his contingency. By this I mean there is no way to encounter Randy without acknowledging the fact that he is dependent on others, so his vulnerability goes before him. In his words, "I'm not looking for a level playing field. If there is a level playing field, I die." When Randy leads people, he acknowledges his (and their) vulnerability in an honest and hopeful way. His presence and teaching not only expose the myth of self-sufficiency, but they de-stabilize dis/ability constructs because the one who is the most vulnerable and dependent physically is in a leadership position. It is clear that his insights/abilities are related to his experience of the world from the position of a motorized wheelchair, as a marginalized person, and as someone whose understanding of vulnerability is experienced corporally. Students are confronted with the fact that leaders can rely on supports and still be effective leaders. Randy's presence and poetry offer a narrative from an insider's perspective (as the marginalized becomes the center) and remind students, faculty, administrators, and anyone who will listen that working for equality and placing hope in enlightened self-interest are not enough to secure the flourishing of people with disabilities. I will let Randy speak for himself.

Term Paper for Louis Kalyvas (A poem by Randy Smit)

I have to get to class, I have to get to church, I have to get to work, I have to

get to a toilet.

Who is getting where on-time? And why—and how exactly. What if you have to go, I mean go go . . . and you have to, you really do and there is no one there to help you in the middle of your carefully crafted lecture on disability?

You have to figure this out. You must learn to master what is fluid. Hold it man,

Control it, man.

Ever hear of moderation? Scheduling is part of life. Everybody has to do it. You don't get special treatment.

How my friend's mother must have wept. Sending him to school

with such oily hair to be stared at, she did her best. His right foot was swollen

twice its size, she did her best, it twisted violently in the bathtub, in a hurry, she did all she could to

get him to school, get him a job, a chance, a way—do it fast, the bus will be here—get him on it, give your weary best, get off your pity porch, you're not the only one struggling.

But Mom—it hurts, it's gonna get worse . . . what if someone bumps it . . .

I have work—you have school—Let's keep going. We've only five minutes. Everyone will be waiting. They will leave without you, they will, they have to, they must. This is how life works. We can't just expect to keep the rest of them waiting.

Time works the same for all of us. Right?

The alarm forces everyone awake the same, into the same culture, the same way of being and doing, it's a kind of fluid we all swim in, right? It's just that some of us are just a little different maybe. Right?

Press on my son, we all say . . . Caffeinate to force it forward, kid, you gotta move it to make it, later on you will not have a chance, a choice. Keep this dream alive my son for when you finally arrive—YOU SHALL LEAD THEM!

in a conversation on demand energy.

[What else can make sense but that they suffer for our teaching?]

Later on in the English teacher's office he will give up pride and ask for an extension, he will confess that at present the term paper is half-baked, not at all what he would want to turn in right now, she will want to help him but if she did that, she says, she would have to do it for everyone and that just wouldn't be fair, and although these choices are tough for her, as much as she would like to, there are even some rabid folks downstairs in the resource room who are pressing her to stick to her guns, she's been told by the able-bodied advocates of these disabled teenagers that this is the only way to see him properly, DO not diminish him!—they say—DO not make him other than anyone of those kids—We know it seems cruel right now but these kids need to learn how to get organized and stay with it and keep pace—nobody's going to hand them their degrees—if you help him like this now, it's only gonna get worse . . . and we have fought too hard and for too long to get him in that room in the first place to give him a chance to compete. . No way, man, stick to your guns. There is

equality to consider, after all.[38]

To reframe Randy's poetic version of a critique of ableist biases in education prosaically, "Concepts of universality and the norm are deeply embedded in academic culture [even seminary and divinity school culture], and can very quickly trigger cries of reverse discrimination, exclusion, or injury from the seemingly displaced group that identifies itself as the norm."[39]

ENABLING WITNESS

How might it look to [dis]able theological formation and enable witness in the specific institutional setting of a seminary? How might the critical engagement of ableist pedagogies open innovative and creative spaces for theology and practice to be enriched? Being a seminary professor, I wonder in what ways Western Theological Seminary can move from being read as "an environment intended for nondisabled persons"[40] to one where people with

---

[38]Randy Smit, "Term Paper for Louis Kalyvas," used with his permission.
[39]James C. Wilson and Cynthia Lewiecki-Wilson, "Constructing a Third Space: Disability Studies, the Teaching of English, and Institutional Transformation," in Snyder, Brueggemann, and Garland-Thomson, *Disability Studies*, 300.
[40]Ibid., 297.

disabilities flourish and where the next generation of Christian leaders includes people with disabilities and others who have been prepared to minister with people with disabilities. Can a seminary nurture the attitudes and
create the structures necessary to sustain such transformation? I believe it
can. Disability scholars Wilson and Lewiecki-Wilson offer three approaches
to changing institutional dynamics that loosely relate to my proposal:
making creative adaptations in the classroom, enhancing access, and representing disability in the classroom.[41] My own proposal involves a comprehensive plan that includes the *presence* of people with disabilities, *intentionally* builds new programs and relationships that ensure disability
concerns are being directly addressed, and includes a strategy to make disability concerns a *dimension* of the course offerings and formative experiences across our entire curriculum.

Presence. Unless people with disabilities are present in religious institutions (churches, parachurch ministries, Christian colleges, graduate theological schools, etc.), they will continue to be objectified and marginalized
(see the Schreiter discussion in the introduction to part two, above), and the
issues raised by the experience of disability will be quarantined as an aspect
of disability concerns rather than acknowledged as an essentially human
concern. Consequently, those institutions will miss out on the embodied
insights and gifts that people with disabilities have to offer.

The authors of *Disability Studies: Enabling the Humanities* suggest, "Disability is indeed a fundamental human experience that is missing from our
critical consciousness."[42] It is likely that, unless people with disabilities are
physically present to challenge teaching practices—changing the rhythm and
dynamics of the classroom, adding their embodied perspectives and voices to
the discussions, including their concerns and joys as a part of the community's
life—then our "critical consciousness" will retain its ableist biases. As Simi
Linton has pointed out, "The embodied perspective of disabled persons . . . is
the necessary ground for realizing the agency of the disabled subject, and it
must be a fundamental part of any curriculum in disability studies" and, I
would add, relevant theological education.[43] While integrating books by

---

[41]Ibid., 300.
[42]Snyder, Brueggemann, and Garland-Thomson, *Disability Studies*, 3.
[43]Linton, quoted in Jim Swan, "Disabilities, Bodies, Voices," in Snyder, Brueggemann, and Garland-
Thomson, *Disability Studies*, 284.

people with disabilities and accounts of people with disabilities into a syllabus adds a voice, such infusion misses out on the confrontation of values and norms that accompanies embodied presence. Brenda Brueggemann, an educator who is hard of hearing, explains that in her literature course she [dis]ables literature by making students aware of how subjects with disabilities are often employed as thin characters to make a literary point in a way that erases the character's personhood. She adds, when this happens, "I'll be standing there, quite unerased, in front of the classroom, gravitating toward whoever is speaking."[44] Robert Anderson, a theological educator, likewise appropriately commends, "People with disabilities offer the wisdom of their embodiment to others. The experience of disability informs our shared understanding of what it means to exist in this world. Where there is no relationship, there can be no voice"; he thereby discerns, "Disability's silence in theological curriculum is related to the relative absence of disabled bodies on campuses."[45]

WTS already has an institutional structure in place that guarantees the presence of people with intellectual and developmental disabilities on campus in Friendship House.[46] Friendship House is a residence where young adults with intellectual disabilities share living quarters with seminary students. The Friend residents hold part-time jobs, volunteer in the community, and meet regularly as a group at weekly Friend time meetings. Beyond that, they are involved in the seminary to the degree that they have interest. Megan hands out bulletins at chapel and frequently attends. Amanda has taken Hebrew and always has something to share during community time after chapel. Seth has helped several professors to introduce seminary students to his experience of Down syndrome. Amanda, Megan, and Seth are impacting the broader seminary community. Their presence changes the dynamic of the classroom, challenges professors' pedagogical practices, and transforms the educational environment. They are challenging reigning assumptions about who is qualified to be a minister and even push the boundaries of our notions of "ministry" and "witness."

[44]Brenda Jo Brueggemann, "An Enabling Pedagogy," in Snyder, Brueggemann, and Garland-Thomson, *Disability Studies*, 318.

[45]Anderson, "In Search of the Disabled Human Body in Theological Education," 50.

[46]For more about the Friendship House at Western Theological Seminary, see Amy Julia Becker, "Roommates and Friends: A Seminary Does Disability Ministry," *Christian Century*, February 6, 2013, www.christiancentury.org/article/2013-02/roommates-and-friends. For more about Friendship House in general, visit www.friendshiphousepartners.com.

While this is a wonderful beginning, we are aware our campus does not fully reflect the diversity of the experience of disability. Aside from Randy's work with the Formation team, there are no people with disabilities in positions of leadership at our seminary. We are imagining and creating and will implement a strategy for recruiting more students with disabilities. In order to create a more hospitable environment for people with disabilities, graduate theological institutions need partners with disabilities and experts in creating inclusive and accessible academic environments to help with evaluating campus facilities, accommodations, and distance-learning platforms in order to make sure they have both physical and social ramps in place. The term "physical ramps" designates alterations to the physical environment to make it more accessible. This includes actual ramps as part of a barrier-free environment, as well as wide doorways, water fountains at various heights, handrails, accessible routes, and all of the other features of a building that are ADA compliant. The term "social ramps" refers to the attitudes and dispositions of people in the institution toward people with disabilities.[47] Physical access to a seminary is meaningless if the person with a disability is never made to feel like he or she belongs. A first priority, therefore, is to execute an accessibility audit of accommodations and disposition.[48]

Along with recruiting more students with disabilities, seminaries should consider hiring professors, visiting professors, or adjunct professors who either have disabilities or have expertise in addressing disability from a theological standpoint. Preferably, these professors will have a disability, but due to the biases inherent in graduate theological education until now, the pool of candidates is small. This has to change, not for the sake of quotas, but for the sake of culture: "It is key that persons with disability be hired not for purpose of tokenism and quotas but to be allies and to center considerations of disability throughout campus sectors. This would potentially reference groups, notions of disability culture and identity and dismantle deficit-based perceptions about what persons with disabilities are

---

[47]See Jeff McNair and Brian McKinney, "Social Ramps: The Principles of Universal Design Applied to the Social Environment," *Journal of the Christian Institute on Disability* 4, no. 1 (Spring/Winter 2015): 43-68.

[48]See, for example, the accessibility audits at "Accessibility Audits," DisAbility Ministries Committee of the United Methodist Church, www.umdisabilityministries.org/access/audit.html.

qualified to accomplish."[49] The presence of professors with disabilities on campus will normalize the idea that people with disabilities can hold leadership positions at a seminary. Importantly, the professors should not be recruited simply to teach adjectival disability courses but also teach in the traditional curriculum in the field of their expertise in order to demonstrate how their unique perspectives as people with disabilities impact their disciplines.

Intention. On December 3, 2014, the International Day of Disabled Persons, the faculty of WTS approved a graduate certificate in disability and ministry (GCDM). The GCDM is a package of credit-bearing, transcriptable courses that can stand alone as a certificate or be rolled into a master of arts or masters of divinity degree. The courses in the GCDM are available in our distance-learning format, so students can stay in their ministry contexts while reflecting theologically with other students and their professor on the implications of the experience of disability for the practice of ministry. The distance-learning platform also allows students with disabilities for whom moving to campus is not possible to have access to the program while allowing students of all abilities to progress through the courses together. Courses are taught by those who are leading the national discussion on disability and ministry, by persons with disabilities, and increasingly by WTS faculty as we develop internal competency and consider how the experience of disability informs our specific disciplines.

The GCDM is one example of how a seminary created a point of intention in the curriculum where disability is addressed directly. Such a program requires continual faculty development and an institutional commitment to maintaining discussions about disability and ministry on campus. Graduate theological institutions must, therefore, develop and deepen relationships with other organizations and individuals that are leaders in disability ministry and theology in order to cultivate conversation partners.

Another possible point of intention could be a lectureship or symposium on disability and ministry. A seminary could inexpensively bring the best scholars with disabilities and those who focus on disability before their faculty and student body. They could also serve local congregations

---

[49]Lauren Shallish, "A Different Diversity? Challenging the Exclusion of Disability Studies from Higher Education Research and Practice," in Kim and Aquino, *Disability as Diversity in Higher Education*, 28.

by offering practice-based workshops in conjunction with the lectures while creating opportunities for our faculty to develop competency relative to disability concerns within their field of expertise.

Dimension. Aside from giving disability an intentional space in the curriculum and community life, seminaries must commit to helping faculty understand and communicate how disability intersects with their disciplinary interests. Since disability is a normal experience of human embodiment, disability studies intersects naturally with the topics addressed across the curriculum in a graduate theological institution. Simi Linton explains the value of disability studies: "A disability studies perspective adds a critical dimension to thinking about issues such as autonomy, competence, wholeness, independence/dependence, health, physical appearance, aesthetics, community, and notions of progress and perfection."[50] Students formed to lead churches that serve as "hermeneutics of the gospel" would call congregations to live in ways that critique powerful cultural assumptions about these very issues (autonomy, wholeness, progress, perfection, etc.) and would greatly benefit from insights from disability studies. By finding partners in disability studies, seminary professors could find the necessary resources to expose ableist biases in their own pedagogy and doctrine and could encourage students to do the same through curriculum infusion or, in the words of Robert Anderson, "interweaving knowledge about the human experience of disability throughout the existing curriculum."[51]

To make disability concerns a dimension of the entire curriculum requires a total community effort and therefore necessitates faculty and staff training. Some of the training can occur implicitly as faculty and staff members spend time with those persons who will join their community as a result of our efforts to increase the presence of people with disabilities on campus. However, other training will necessarily be more focused and could be specifically offered as part of wider cultural competency training. Disability needs to be recast in terms of diversity or multicultural expression. Robert Anderson has suggested, "Exposure to disability inquiry and 'culture' broadens a theological school's capacity to

---

[50]Linton, Mello, and O'Neill, "Disability Studies: Expanding the Parameters of Diversity," 5.
[51]Anderson, "Infusing the Graduate Theological Curriculum with Education About Disability," 147.

become more inclusive. In effect, theological students have opportunities for more informed contextual learning experiences—about the world, people with disabilities, and themselves."[52] Cultural competency training involves discerning a person's cultural awareness and attitudes toward and assumptions about similarities and differences, recognizing personally held and culturally situated biases, and determining one's motivation and ability to engage cultural diversity, as well as considering concrete strategies for engaging cultural encounters with individuals and groups from diverse settings. Such training is a natural setting for people to consider disability and could help people to see the generative potential rather than possible barriers that accompany including disability perspectives.

An appropriate response to theologically rich cultural competency training will likely require changes to theology, biblical hermeneutics, liturgical life, and congregational practices and, importantly, change on the part of the self.[53] Cultural competency training at a seminary is less about conveying methods and techniques for creating a hospitable environment than it is about experiencing the kind of personal transformation that makes us better able to love through the Christian practice of hospitality.[54]

A CHALLENGE: INCLUDING PEOPLE WITH INTELLECTUAL DISABILITY IN GRADUATE THEOLOGICAL EDUCATION

Ian Dickson, principal of Belfast Bible College, notes how the primary genre of education at theological schools is rational learning—which is not all that different from other colleges and universities. He posits that people with intellectual disabilities might be agents of change for theological institutions, opening educators and students to creative disruption and providing a challenge to both "our rootedness in word-culture and our boundaries of inclusion."[55] Rather than simply offering courses about intellectual disability, he imagines all courses being challenged at their core by including

---

[52]Anderson, "In Search of the Disabled Human Body in Theological Education," 43.

[53]Robert J. Schreiter, "Teaching Theology from an Intercultural Perspective," *Theological Education* 26, no. 1 (1989): 19.

[54]For an excellent study in the difference between the technique or instrumental use of hospitality and the practice of hospitality see Christine D. Pohl, *Making Room: Recovering Hospitality as a Christian Tradition* (Grand Rapids: Eerdmans, 1999).

[55]J. N. Ian Dickson, "Unexpected Revolutionaries: Reflections on Intellectual Disability," *The Theological Educator* 4, no. 2 (2011): 33.

the presence of people with disabilities. Where teaching about intellectual disability can create an environment where "our sacredness and spirituality, our humanness and vulnerability, our pomposity and elitism rise to the surface to mix and clash and recreate us,"[56] taking the spiritual lives of people with disabilities seriously may prove an exercise that transforms our very understanding of who is a theologian and what it means to be spiritual in ways that are accessible to persons beyond those with disabilities. Dickson explains, with insight developed as a practical theologian, "If, for example, in contrast to the view that spiritual experience comes out of our theological understanding (requiring sophisticated cognitive ability), we come to understand theology as reflection on our spiritual experience (an experience that does not necessarily require a theological understanding and articulation of that understanding to make it valid) then Christianity becomes accessible to persons with intellectual disability."[57]

We must have the presence of people with disabilities in our community and classrooms if we expect all students to be transformed in such understandings as I have explained above. Dickson agrees: "We as theological educators need to be informed by the presence of intellectually disabled students whose whole life, attitude and requirements are so different from our own."[58] Why are people with intellectual disabilities not considered potential students at theological seminaries? Is there nothing they could gain from participating in courses and seminars? Do they have nothing to offer the educational and formative process of preparing men and women to lead the church in ministry and mission? Dickson asks, "Could it be that God is calling us at this time to rethink what constitutes theological intelligence, to give access to the 'unlikely' shapers of our future and to pioneer forms of training for theological formation so that no one is forgotten?"[59]

CONCLUSION

In their insightful essay "Constructing a Third Space: Disability Studies, the Teaching of English, and Institutional Transformation," James Wilson and

---

[56]Ibid.
[57]Ibid., 35.
[58]Ibid.
[59]Ibid., 36.

Cynthia Lewiecki-Wilson offer a challenge to educational institutions: "We urge others to think about how disabled and nondisabled people might reimagine the spatial, cultural, and intellectual landscape of the academy through an encounter with disability and how this academic transformation might contribute to the remaking of other social spaces."[60] The direct implications for a seminary are obvious—in order to reimagine our formative landscape from the perspective of an encounter with disability, disability must be present in our spaces, curricula, and hermeneutics in the form of people with disabilities and their voices—even if they are not audible. Second, we need to consider how the environment we create in the seminary can "contribute to the remaking of other social space," specifically the churches and ministries in which our students will lead and participate. In order to change the seminary's environment or culture, we will need intentional spaces in the curriculum and on campus to address these issues, and we will need disability concerns to be a dimension of the entire curriculum. We need to help students to imagine how a disability viewpoint can offer them a perspective from which they can engage afresh and in animating ways issues of embodiment, social and political dynamics, pedagogy, and Christian formation for the sake of a more credible Christian witness in the world.

---

[60]Wilson and Lewiecki-Wilson, "Constructing a Third Space," 297.

Epilogue

Enabling Witness

More than 25 percent of American families have at least one relative with a disability.[1] The experience of finding oneself, a family member, or a friend closer to the "dis-" side of the dis/ability spectrum at some point in life is an unremarkable feature of human existence. Disability can provide a perspective—a point of reference, a kind of hermeneutical advantage—for more fully understanding the human condition *as people actually experience it* and, relatedly, for refining Christian theology, reconsidering pastoral practices, and cultivating a more credible witness in the world. In other words, when we [dis]able Christian ministry and witness—by which I mean divest it of ableist biases and open it to the full range of human embodiments, capacities, and modes of communication—we enable witness.

Hans Reinders, in his explication of Jean Vanier's theology, explains Vanier's understanding of "the essence of Christian witness" in the following terms: "the people on whom our world has turned its back reveal the mystery of Jesus."[2] The revelation of Jesus provides the necessary contrast for revealing certain things about our society and us. The presence and perspective of people with disabilities, when attended to through the lens of this gospel, can help the church to unmask cultural biases against all kinds of embodiments, physical and intellectual variances, and mental health differences. Such biases unchecked sustain interpretations that authenticate values that, in turn, support the oppression of people with disabilities in the church and beyond and squelch our witness. Judith Roberts writes, "Discipleship

---

[1]Qi Wang, *Disability and American Families: 2000* (Washington, DC: U.S. Census Bureau, 2000).
[2]Hans S. Reinders, "Being with the Disabled: Jean Vanier's Theological Realism," in *Disability in the Christian Tradition: A Reader*, ed. Brian Brock and John Swinton (Grand Rapids: Eerdmans, 2012), 468.

with the marginalized at the centre calls the church to acknowledge the brokenness and sin that preserves systems that produce inequities in church and society."[3] When congregations acknowledge the subtle ways that they exclude the contributions of people with disabilities from the church and become awakened to the disproportionate impact incarceration, unemployment, homelessness, and abuse have on persons with disabilities and then align themselves with Jesus, who aligned himself with the marginalized, they are participating in Christian witness in a way that is transforming to both society and the church.

In the previous chapters I presented an introduction to disability informed by disability studies with the intention of complexifying commonsense understandings of disability for the sake of reengaging the concept through the lens of mission studies. Throughout the book, I have attempted to demonstrate ways that mission studies and disability studies can work synergistically to enable witness. In this work of Christian missiology, I admitted from the start and emphasize now that the most important enabling for Christian witness is the enabling power of the Holy Spirit. However, concepts from missiology such as *missio Dei*, indigenization and contextualization, and witness are also important for liberating and amplifying marginalized voices. Additionally, readings of mission history that privilege the activity and perspectives of people with disabilities can stimulate the imagination of pastors and parishioners to see disabilities in terms of gains instead of primarily in terms of losses. Such re-engagements of mission history and theology can provide models and visions of Christian witness that "measure up to the heights and depths of the human situation."[4]

---

[3]Judith E. B. Roberts, "Discipleship with the Marginalized at the Centre," *International Review of Mission* 103, no. 2 (2014): 191.

[4]Lesslie Newbigin, "Not Whole Without the Handicapped," in *Partners in Life: The Handicapped and the Church*, ed. Geiko Müller-Fahrenholz (Geneva: WCC Publications, 1979), 24.

Author Index

Subject Index

theological anthropology, 29, 103, 107-8, 110-11, 116, 120-23, 144

theological education, 6-9, 61, 143-45, 147, 150, 154, 156, 161

theōsis, 124, 126, 132, 134, 137

therapeutic riding, 2

trans-ability, 25

unemployment, 27, 33, 170

Union Theological Seminary/Union Presbyterian Seminary, 14

vocation, 75, 108, 116, 122, 139

Western Theological Seminary, 1, 15, 146, 154, 157, 159, 161

wheelchair user, 13, 17, 19

Willowbrook State School, 105

witness, 2-9, 12, 18, 26-27, 33, 35-41, 44, 45, 47-62, 67, 71, 79-80, 92-95, 101-4, 108, 113-14, 116, 122-27, 129, 130-34, 136-41, 144, 146-47, 150, 153-54, 159, 162, 169-70

Christian, 4, 8, 27, 39, 47-48, 50, 54-56, 123-24, 131, 167, 169-70

World Autism Day, 28

World Council of Churches (WCC), 34, 39, 55-57, 131, 137, 148

World Health Organization (WHO), 18, 25

MISSIOLOGICAL ENGAGEMENTS

Series Editors: Scott W. Sunquist,
Amos Yong, and John R. Franke

Missiological Engagements: Church, Theology, and Culture in Global Contexts charts interdisciplinary and innovative trajectories in the history, theology, and practice of Christian mission at the beginning of the third millennium.

Among its guiding questions are the following: What are the major opportunities and challenges for Christian mission in the twenty-first century? How does the missionary impulse of the gospel reframe theology and hermeneutics within a global and intercultural context? What kind of missiological thinking ought to be retrieved and reappropriated for a dynamic global Christianity? What innovations in the theology and practice of mission are needed for a renewed and revitalized Christian witness in a postmodern, postcolonial, postsecular, and post-Christian world?

Books in the series, both monographs and edited collections, will feature contributions by leading thinkers representing evangelical, Protestant, Roman Catholic, and Orthodox traditions, who work within or across the range of biblical, historical, theological, and social-scientific disciplines. Authors and editors will include the full spectrum from younger and emerging researchers to established and renowned scholars, from the Euro-American West and the Majority World, whose missiological scholarship will bridge church, academy, and society.

Missiological Engagements reflects cutting-edge trends, research, and innovations in the field that will be of relevance to theorists and practitioners in churches, academic domains, mission organizations, and NGOs, among other arenas.

Finding the Textbook You Need

The IVP Academic Textbook Selector
is an online tool for instantly finding the IVP books
suitable for over 250 courses across 24 disciplines.